Don Rosenthal performed witl
before ending his professional (
living there in a remote cabin
years and, after living rustica
where Don became a counsello
northern Vermont. They give workshops internationally on intimate relationship. In addition Don has a private counselling
practice helping others to heal and awaken.

Martha Rosenthal taught in a number of elementary schools
before leaving her profession to live alone in Alaska. She went
on to study body work and developed a private practice. After
moving to Vermont, Martha extended her practice to include
counselling of individuals and couples. She also gives workshops for women, in addition to couples workshops with Don.

INTIMACY

THE NOBLE ADVENTURE

Don & Martha Rosenthal

The Collins Press

Published in 1999 by
The Collins Press
West Link Park
Doughcloyne
Wilton
Cork

British Library Cataloguing in Publication data.

Typesetting by The Collins Press Ltd.

Jacket design by Artmark.

Printed in Ireland by Colour Books Ltd.

ISBN: 1-898256-77-2

CONTENTS

FOREWORD

by Simon & Stephen Pearce

Don and Martha Rosenthal seem to dedicate most of their waking moments to exploring intimacy in relationship to one another and anyone else who is willing to beat down the briars on this less trodden path.

Kim-Mai and I first met Don and Martha in four feet of snow at a warm isolated house in Vermont. My brother Simon and his wife, Pia, had recently taken part in 'The Noble Adventure', Don and Martha's weekend, where in a safe and loving environment couples can develop the skills which lead towards greater intimacy. They told us it was the most important thing they had ever done in their lives.

One of my chief preoccupations is learning what this game of life is about, and I have searched in some pretty unique places.

Whenever I look deeply at myself I have an almost paralysing thrill which starts in my tummy and permeates my whole body and mind. I suspect that Formula One drivers and bungy jumpers have the same sensation. So when we were driving to meet Don and Martha, I hoped the car would break down and maybe we wouldn't be able to find the house ...

As the weekend finished I was very grateful to Simon and Pia for recommending that we go there. It is very difficult to put into words one of those rare moments where the 'earth moves'. Mostly it was pretty simple stuff, but the results and implications for everyday life were enormous.

My abiding memory of leaving Don and Martha, after the initial encounter, was that the work we had done and the humanity we had shared were not unusual on an absolute scale, yet the feelings and insights were unusual in the context of our lives, and deep down I felt well qualified to follow this new path. It was as if I was being reminded of something that my deepest intelligence was already aware of. The overall experience was one of coming home and not of setting off for uncharted territories.

Kim-Mai and I have spent a good deal of time, on more than ten occasions over the past five years, working with Don and Martha, and our time together has been some of the most fulfilling of my present life.

As a man I would like to talk a bit about Don. Don does not set himself up as a guru. He does not pretend to know the answers to the conundrum of the human condition, but he certainly directs a lot of energy towards looking and living his intuition.

Don started his adult life as a classical musician touring the world. For more than thirty years Don has concentrated exclusively on his enquiry into the human condition, consciousness, intimacy, relationship, being present in the moment, all of the material which has occupied the mystics since time began – if there is any time.

Don's greatest concern is that we should use our path of enquiry as an opportunity to communicate and become intimate. The whole process of life is about having close meaningful relationships (of every kind – me and the taxi driver, you and your bank manager and particularly me and my lover). Don might contend, and I would agree, that most of life is spent trying to control things, which is the opposite to surrender and intimacy.

I have walked on glaciers in Iceland with Don. I have shared my brother's hot tub with all six of us. I have spent eight days fasting with my wife and Don. We have cried, laughed and been terrified by our own selves.

I see this book as a working manual, a distillation of a wise and loving man's experience, written to share with all of us who have the time to stop and wonder what is really going on.

I cannot over-recommend Don and Martha's weekend workshop 'The Noble Adventure', as a place to fall in love with yourself and your partner. Don't wait until you hit pot holes in your relationship, though it works for that too. Treat yourself. Celebrate life in the bosom of Don and Martha's love.

Once you have experienced 'the work' first hand this book will stand out in 3-D.

I keep this book beside my bed at all times and if my mind is racing I open it at random. Like any truth it does not matter where you begin. The book is a guide book to the treasures that we own but rarely take out to polish.

Don and Martha are not here to answer your questions – they are here as male and female touchstones, each sharing both qualities. They are here to help us find our path and our truth and they are extraordinarily dedicated to this loving work.

While the theme of *Intimacy* is intimacy and interaction, almost one-third of the book concerns learning about, living with and loving oneself. As Don says 'it is much harder to become intimate with and communicate with other people if one does not know, love and understand oneself. For me, I am finding that as I begin to have more of a feel for myself, so too do I become better at intimacy and more adept at running my business and understanding the other people who work with me.' So intimacy is not just for lovers.

I used to think I was a modern man dedicated to the emancipation of women. Then I found outdated bits of old-fashioned male in me which deeply fears womanhood. While learning to love this part of me I have been very grateful for Don and Martha's steady hand.

I think the war of the sexes will always be with us. I know Don and Martha would like to see a lasting peace. I agree with them that it is possible but I am painfully aware of my own tendencies.

Please indulge yourself in reading of Don and Martha's work and let your intelligence see what you find in this treasure chest.

STEPHEN PEARCE, 1999

If you are just glancing through this book trying to decide whether it's of interest to you and whether you should buy it or not, all you need to do is ask yourself whether or not you are really interested in relationships. Because if you are interested in relationships, don't even think about not buying this book.

I think I have known Don and Martha for about five years and I can say, without hesitation, that they have radically changed my life for the better.

I can also say I don't believe I would still be with my wife were it not for Don and Martha, and not only are we still together, but it feels like our relationship is just beginning. I have discovered what intimacy is. I have discovered what it feels like to deeply love someone else. I have discovered what it feels like to choose love over fear.

I am not saying it's always wonderful and that we don't have our down times. Of course we do. We are still learning and we are human, but the down times are much less often and we are much better equipped to get over them, thanks to the work we have done with Don and Martha – which is described in this book.

Thank you Don and Martha for your extraordinary gift and commitment to this work and to all of us who want to share our lives with someone else.

SIMON PEARCE, 1999

INTRODUCTION

Martha and I began our relationship in a small, spartan cabin in the Katchemak Wilderness Area in South Central Alaska. There were no roads; we had to take a boat about eight miles to the nearest town once a month for supplies.

Our life was simple. We gathered wood, took walks and did yoga. We sat in stillness by the window and watched it get light and dark. In the plentiful northern winter darkness we had long, deep talks by kerosene light. Peacefulness arose in following ancient rhythms, as we attempted to come upon simplicity and balance after years of stressful living.

Lacking outside pressure, we found ourselves getting along quite well for our first few years. Fights and unpleasant exchanges were alien to us, and in their absence we thought we had really attained something special. In fact, our unusual lifestyle had allowed us to fabricate an a positive image of our relationship that was unrealistic.

After five years of living this way we realised it was time for a dramatic change. A sameness had crept into our rhythms, and with a lack of newness the quiet life began feeling more like stagnation than serenity. It was time to try something different. We ended up in a small coastal village in Northern California, where we gradually entered into a more traditional (relatively speaking – it was still California!) lifestyle.

All of a sudden the precious peace we had so carefully crafted together was shattered. In the abrupt influx of new people, ideas, experiences, stresses, we found ourselves not only noticing flaws in each other but becoming increasingly disturbed by what we saw. As a result, over time, each of us closed down to the other emotionally and sexually, while the other responded in kind. Within two years we hit bottom. Many a simple exchange erupted into a painful and seemingly pointless fight. The kindness and tenderness were gone. Neither of us felt emotionally safe with the other and the mutual trust had evaporated. Something felt terribly wrong. Where had the love gone? How could this have happened?

Today, over twenty years later, we still observe friends and acquaintances repeating our problems. A truly flowering intimacy is apparently most elusive. Even those of intelligence, integrity and goodwill are finding that their education and experience has not taught them enough to keep intimacy flourishing. Those who take their spiritual lives seriously are not immune from the sometimes breathtaking difficulties of being intimate. Couples of every persuasion, from the most traditional to the most 'new age' have the same trouble feeling and expressing the love they originally felt between them. Others, alone and scarred from the battlefield of relationship, seriously wonder if such an ongoing bond is even possible.

Martha and I did survive our crisis, and have found a depth of connection that we never could have imagined. We have gone through many moments of joyous discovery, and have committed many a painful blunder. In confronting our difficulties we have made full use of the meditative pursuits we assimilated in our cabin days, as well as various Eastern and Western spiritual teachings, some Western psychology, and a great deal of groping in our blindness. Although we still have our difficult moments, we are deeply grateful for the love we now have together and would like to share with you, in the following pages, what has made it possible.

chapter 1

WHAT GOES WRONG

WHAT HOLDS RELATIONSHIPS TOGETHER?

WHAT is the force that holds couples together? In earlier days it was mutual dependance, economic necessity and social/religious pressure. Most remained together for a lifetime, although few were able to reach across the formidable barriers of traditional male and female role models, to make a genuine connection. In fact, few had any vision of what true intimacy might look like.

The 1960s turned things around. The women's movement, sexual revolution, and the abandonment by many of traditional religious thinking largely demolished the notion that couples should stay together through all kinds of difficulty. As a society we searched desperately for a new purpose in being together. Many hoped to find it in the sexual and emotional gratification of the early phase of romance.

As we enter into intimacy most of us feel an incompleteness in our being. It is tempting to regard our intimacy as a means to

1

fill this vast emptiness. We hope to receive uninterrupted positive attention and a continually passionate and exciting sexual experience. What even allows us to believe in such a patent impossibility is the presence of these qualities for a brief period during the early, romantic phase of the relationship. Thus encouraged, we set up an image in our mind of a relationship whose continual, positive and passionate qualities keep us from experiencing our loneliness. Our union is now held together by the hope of uninterrupted mutual gratification.

This unrealistic desire leads to inevitable disillusionment. Anyone who enters into intimacy with the purpose of mutual gratification is embarking on a path of pain. Nobody is capable of keeping us perpetually satisfied; another person cannot rescue us from our demons. Should we fall into this common trap of mutually expecting each other to keep us happy, the futility of our arrangement will become quickly apparent. Each will commonly begin to resent the other for not fulfilling their impossible task. A new phase of relationship begins, where both partners experience a growing negativity they are sorely unequipped to handle.

UNWORKABLE STRATEGIES

Living with another person brings us face-to-face with our deepest layers of inner disturbance, dating back to childhood. These disturbances are mental habits that create illusion, close the heart, and interfere with feeling and expressing love. Nothing reveals these inner habits as forcefully as intimacy.

For most of us, these habits bring hurt, anger, and other painful feelings as an inevitable accompaniment to intimacy. Though the feelings are inevitable, how we respond will determine whether they erode the foundations of love and trust, or whether they become the raw material for greater understanding and compassion.

2

Most of us have not developed the special skills needed to respond wisely to the powerful negative feelings that intimacy awakens. When conflicts arise we tend to react largely from conditioning and habit.

In our early years we develop certain survival strategies which help us to respond to the difficulties of our family life. These methods of coping become programmed deeply into our mind, where they remain in the depths of our conscious. They may control our behaviour for a lifetime, unless released through understanding.

Although many types of strategy abound, they can be broken down into three traditional forms. You may recognise one or more of the styles as your own.

Niceness

Do you put on a 'nice' face, and attempt to find love by transcending or denying negativity? Those who employ this strategy avoid conflict by making peace at all costs. In order not to create disturbance they are willing to sacrifice their integrity.

Those who favour 'niceness' need to become familiar with the way they deny their truth. Their work is to embrace uncomfortable feelings as an acceptable part of life. It may require courage, for example, to express anger, and wisdom to do so at the right time with an open heart.

Withdrawal

Do you withdraw behind an emotional barrier and attempt to find peace by not allowing pain into conscious awareness? Men in particular admire and emulate the stoic hero of the Western movie, the classic example of one who puts his feelings aside because it seems safer not to feel. An emotional numbness results, or a loss of aliveness.

Those who withdraw from feeling must learn how to move their energy, perhaps through guided expression of anger or pain. They, too, require the courage to get in touch with all their feelings, and learn that it is safe to express them.

3

Aggressive Behaviour

Do you feel a sense of power and control when you are being aggressive? If you employ this approach you tend to lash out at your partner, continually finding fault, picking fights and blaming the other for all that isn't right. The result is weariness from so much emotional turmoil, and guilt for being such a difficult partner. In addition one's mate tends to close down out of self-protection, and a loss of trust results.

Those who explode in blame and anger need to find alternative, less harmful outlets for their emotional intensity. They will also benefit from questioning more fully the beliefs that lead to the blaming of others for their own pain.

'Niceness', withdrawal, and aggressive behaviour are unsatisfactory because they avoid dealing directly with difficult feelings. Pretending everything is OK, hiding behind a wall, or lashing out in attack, are painfully ineffective ways of communicating that inevitably fail to bring resolution. But we are faced with a difficult challenge: our strategies have become so deeply ingrained that they tend to remain for a lifetime, unless we work to release them. Only those who are able to transcend their strategies will have an opportunity to experience an intimacy that flourishes over time. Much of this book deals directly or indirectly with the releasing of these habitual and inadequate ways of responding to conflict and pain.

THE DOWNWARD SPIRAL: HOW RELATIONSHIPS FALL APART

Through the years we have worked with hundreds of couples who, like us, originally perceived the purpose of their relationship as mutual gratification. Eventually one party would fail to gratify, for which the partner would resent them, since they were not fulfilling the function they had been assigned. The partner would express their resentment unskilfully, and the painful downward spiral began its inevitable course.

4

Whenever we perceive our partner to be looking unkindly on us, unless we are extremely alert, we react. We close down, defend ourselves, and we even go on the offensive. A variety of negative thoughts and emotions may arise at this point: hurt, anger, anxiety, judgement, resentment, confusion ... anything but love.

If our purpose in being intimate is merely to feel good, this unpleasantness is seen as an annoying and regrettable obstacle, to be pushed away or overcome. If we believe our partner's role is to make us comfortable or whole, then whenever they are not fulfilling this function, we resent them. In so doing we are not helping them to feel comfortable or whole, and the feeling swiftly becomes mutual.

Negative feelings are now breeding an increasing resentment that feeds on itself. As imperfections arise, each partner begins to resent the other for not being the perfect, radiant, loving person whom they experienced at the beginning.

Traits which were initially admired may now seem less attractive. The pristine honesty for which we once esteemed our partner has now come to appear a blunt and tactless disregard for our feelings. Or their childlike spontaneity may have become a childish and immature emotional indulgence. Or their rock-like steadiness and reliability may now feel more like a drab and lacklustre predictability, lacking in passion and vitality.

This change in perception leads to a loss of affection. The sweet little gestures that so naturally accompanied the romantic stage wither away. The tone of voice now begins to acquire an edge. The once exciting sexuality takes on a more mechanical quality. As the downward spiral deepens, fights or withdrawal become more frequent, and the quality of kindness begins to wither away. As each feels more misunderstood it becomes increasingly difficult to see what in their partner initially attracted them.

Every loveless act in one partner generates a further negative reaction in the other. The fear of losing what was so precious increases mutual fear. Guilt, too, is generated. Each partner, observing themselves becoming more difficult to be around, likes themselves less and less in the presence of the other. The increasing guilt intensifies the discomfort level in the relationship, and may lead to further hostility or avoidance. Now the classic downward spiral is in full force.

Since our education has taught us virtually nothing about this prevalent and painful phenomenon, we are totally unprepared to respond when it arises. We find ourselves getting drawn into a process that feels out of our control, as the dream begins to crumble.

Left unchecked to run its course, the downward spiral results either in the relationship blowing apart, or in a lifetime permeated with resentment. Couples who remain together in the midst of such bitterness end up either quarrelling and fighting endlessly, or surviving by putting an emotional callous around the negativity. This most common 'solution' to the problem of resentment results in a relationship without joy or passion, one which is essentially dead. If their original purpose was mutual gratification, few couples escape these painful consequences.

THE PSYCHOLOGICAL MISTAKE

To arrest this downward spiral it is necessary to learn a more effective response when our partner is not pleasing us. Waiting for the change to come from our partner is a fruitless endeavour; the responsibility for change has to come from oneself. But if you have tried, you well know that altering the way you respond to negativity is no easy task.

In addition to our personal strategies for dealing with conflict, our culture has provided us with two approaches, one psychologically based, the other spiritually. Each of these approaches contains an important truth, yet each is fatally flawed. It will be helpful to look more closely at these common ways of responding to difficulty in intimacy.

We call the first the psychological mistake. It originates from seeing the need to accept ourselves just the way we are, to avoid a continual state of denial and conflict. We cannot push away our self-centredness, resentment, or other 'undesirable' feelings and change them simply by an act of will. In fact, no inner or outer manipulation, however subtle, will bring fundamental change.

This perspective emphasises the limitation of living according to 'shoulds'. When we find ourselves getting angry or resentful towards our partner, we refuse to suppress these feelings. We are encouraged to get angry, to cry, to relive old hurts, to express our frustration with our partner.

However, this approach is flawed by its lack of vision. There is little interest in going beyond these negative feelings; in fact spiritual aspirations are seen as an escape from the real world. The psychological mistake unquestioningly assumes that our partner's negative behaviour is an actual threat, rather than a perceived one. Therefore our unloving feelings and defensiveness are fully justified.

At its worst the psycholgical mistake encourages indulgence of negative feelings and righteous judgement towards the imperfections of one's partner. It is possible to spend years in therapy honing one's blaming apparatus. We become highly skilful at identifying what doesn't feel good, getting in touch with and giving full expression to anger and hurt. In fact we may enjoy this indulgence on a regular and frequent basis.

The problem with the psycholgical approach is that we can spend a lifetime luxuriating in the pleasure of negative feelings and never come to the end of it. We are tempted to lay our difficulties at the feet of others, to enjoy the role of victim, denying our own contribution as an adult to the way we feel. We have failed to call into question the hidden attitudes that give rise to our negative feelings and perpetuate them.

Perhaps more importantly, this indulgence strengthens and solidifies some profoundly mistaken notions that lie at the root of our pain. By blaming others for our suffering and remaining complacent about our own responsibilites, we fail to investigate the real purpose of our distress. The uncomfortable outcome is a relationship where unexamined blaming of the other becomes a way of life. Therefore the psychological mistake keeps us feeling powerless, afraid and resentful of the people we think are responsible for our pain. Something of profound importance is missing here.

THE SPIRITUAL MISTAKE

What is missing can be found in its antithesis, the spiritual mistake, although this perspective also has its own limitation. It originates from seeing the true need to go beyond the petty concerns of the daily mind, to transcend self-centredness, anger and violence.

Deep in our being lurks a sense that we have the right and the capablity to experience love, peace, and joy in this lifetime. Why remain content with the grey world of guilt and fear, or with the superficial pleasures with which we escape our pain? Our discontent with all this is telling us something very real that needs to be honoured. It tells us that we need to live by a vision of something more lofty. We don't have to live out our lives in the prison of fear we have crafted for ourselves. Fundamental change is possible.

Those who hold this vision of going beyond the prison of daily life try as hard as they can to live up to ideals such as forgiveness, a positive attitude, and acceptance of their partner 'just as they are'. The spiritual traditions all state that we should obey the Golden Rule, forgive, be charitable and kind to others, even to those who are unkind to us. A perfect state is held up, in contrast to our present imperfection, and we are exhorted to make an effort, gross or subtle, to become that. If at present our heart is closed, if we are unforgiving, angry, agitated, self-centred, we are

8

asked to envision a state – always in the future – in which our heart is open, we are forgiving, peaceful, quiet of mind, loving. We make a supreme effort to have good thoughts and emotions, as well as right actions. We are virtuous if we succeed, sinful if we fail. As an inducement to make this shift, rewards or punishments, in this life or the next, are sometimes offered.

A major difficulty with this approach is that we want so much to be 'good', to transcend our humanness, that we are tempted to deny the darker aspects of our actual emotional reality. For example, many of us as children were told that big boys (or girls) don't cry. Our sadness was denied, but it was certainly not dispelled. What is not first accepted cannot be transformed. You can never get rid of a feeling by denying or resisting it, by saying that it's bad and you shouldn't have it. Although we may try to hide these less savoury facets of our inner life, they have not disappeared and they remain to haunt us from beneath.

The attempt to live up to spiritual ideals presents another common difficulty. To the extent that we take our spiritual progress seriously, we harbour fear, often unconsciously, that we won't succeed in our transformation. This fear gives rise to an act of harsh self-judgement every time we fail to live up to our ideal. And in addition, this lack of charity towards ourselves will often cause us to close our hearts to those who, like us, are not able to attain our lofty ideals of spiritual perfection.

Without accepting our human imperfections we end up judging them when they arise in ourselves or in others. We fail to realise that the very act of judgement is another act of violence, an example of the very thing we our judging. To achieve a peaceful and loving end we are employing a means that is repressive and unkind. When we deny our humanness in the interest of transcending it, we far too often foster those very qualities of separation, closed-heartedness and self-centredness that we find so distasteful.

This perhaps may help to explain why, after so many thousands of years of high-minded teachings, we seem largely unable to live up to these noble-sounding dictums, especially with the person we claim to love most in the world. How many of us, when our partner is upset with us, are actually able to put into practice the great and supremely difficult teaching of responding to negativity with love? Anyone who has tried to do this will acknowledge that it is far easier to appreciate the beauty of the teaching from a safe distance than actually to put it in practice.

Denial is the end product of making certain feelings unacceptable. The spiritual mistake breeds relationships filled with indirect expressions of repressed negativity, which seriously impedes communication about important issues.

After Martha and I reached our lowest point we tried everything we could, falling frequently into one or the other of these mistakes. At times we became experts at the righteous expression of negativity. At other times we tried heroically to relate from a more enlightened perspective, pretending to an equanimity that was sorely lacking. Of course neither helped. We seemed so thoroughly unable to give each other what we thought we wanted that we came very close to ending our relationship.

But something kept us going. Perhaps it was our shared passion for finding a path that would allow ample expression of all our feelings, even the most negative, while at the same time preserving a loving space in which both of us felt safe. We wanted to bring together heaven and earth, as it were, keeping the vision in the midst of the chaos. Sometimes it has felt like walking along a narrow ridge with a precipice on each side. After struggling for years, with many victories and setbacks, we have come to see that there is another way of responding to difficult feelings that neither represses nor indulges them, but allows them to be transformed to something higher.

THE NEW PURPOSE IN BEING TOGETHER

We come back now to our quest for the new purpose that will succeed in holding couples together despite the sizeable difficulties. An approach is needed that will allow couples to go through hurt, anger, fear, confusion and conflict, and somehow manage to emerge with their relationship not only intact, but deeper.

We feel that what will hold couples lovingly together is a shared vision of relationship as a spiritual path. This vision will bring together what is best from both the psychological and the spiritual approaches. Much of this book is an elaboration of what this means in actual practice.

The process involves a fundamental shift in the relationship's centre of gravity. No longer is our purpose in being together simply the serving of our individual needs. Our relationship is no longer a bargain of convenience.

Our joint purpose is to find the truth of who we really are by bringing compassion, awareness and honesty into every aspect of our relationship and our daily life. In discovering together what blocks our love, we open ourselves to higher possibilities. Instead of being antagonists in a power struggle, we become allies in a journey of exploration. When there is conflict, instead of each struggling against the other, the two of us have become allies in a common struggle against old patterns of fear, blame and unconsciousness. We also join forces in struggling together with habits that engender disharmony, at the physical, emotional, mental, or spiritual levels. Whoever is the more aware in the moment can lead the way. If our light goes out we will temporarily borrow our partner's, and vice versa. The old struggle tore us apart; the new struggle strengthens our bond.

In pursuit of this quest we learn that change comes not through effort and resistance, but through understanding. We learn to hone our awareness when we would normally be mechanical, to open the heart when we are traditionally judgemental. We learn to look upon all anger, hurt, and fear-based behaviours – our own or our partner's – as a cry for healing and help rather than as a threat to our safety or a reflection of our unworthiness. We learn a radically new way of communicating that enables the release of defensiveness in the interest of our true safety. We create an emotionally safe environment in which we facilitate the healing of old wounds. We do all this because we have embraced a spiritual vision that aspires to something better and nobler, yet has room for our imperfections. This is a profound and significant challenge. Neither our parents, our schools, nor even our religions, have adequately prepared us.

THE RIGHT USE OF DIFFICULTIES

A great mass of fear lurks in the human consciousness. Perhaps each of us has taken on our own piece of it to process and release. To facilitate this work some of us have chosen a partner to help us discover more clearly where our understanding is incomplete.

It is hard to understand that there can be negative energy between your partner and yourself without there being anything wrong, or anyone to blame. When a relationship becomes a spiritual path, we are no longer interested in blaming our partner if things are not feeling comfortable. Being comfortable is no longer our chief goal. Our purpose, instead of gratification and pleasure, is to help each other unearth and work through anything that might be blocking the full expression of our essence.

All the difficulties between us can be used to reach our new goal. Troublesome feelings are feedback, pointing, if we know how to look, to the places in both that are in need of light, of clarity, of a new way of seeing.

We sense that at some level we have asked for these difficulties as a teaching to show us our obstacles. Therefore in our depths we are grateful to each other for everything, comfortable or otherwise, that helps us to see the truth about ourselves. Knowing ourselves frees us from the illusion which has kept us in a state of pain and conflict.

PAIN AS FEEDBACK

How, then, do we begin to change our attitude towards uncomfortable feelings? The use of pain as feedback is perhaps easiest to understand at the physical level. Hangovers taught me a great deal in my heavy drinking days; in fact they kept me from succumbing fully to alcoholism at a relatively early age. If I have a terrible headache every Sunday morning, it is useful to regard this as a piece of feedback, directing me to look at what I was putting into my system every Saturday night. A hangover is a very direct, specific, non-verbal message, a piece of feedback from my body. It is nothing other than an invitation to investigate.

Toxins can assume many forms. I also carry psychological toxins within my mind: mistaken values, beliefs or attitudes, out of harmony with the way my mind was meant to function.

It has been said, 'The truth will set you free; but first it will make you miserable'. Psychological toxins, like hangovers, give rise to a suffering which is asking something of me. The physical discomfort of the hangover was an invitation to investigate on the physical plane; the mental discomfort in my relationship is an invitation to investigate on the psychological plane.

A typical psychological toxin might be the belief that when my partner expresses anger I am in danger. But what if my discomfort arises not from their behaviour, but rather from the fact that I am regarding it through a powerfully distorted lens? What if I were to take all the energy I had been using to blame my partner, and use it to explore how my mind suffers through its interpretation of her anger?

It takes courage to face yourself, to look unflinchingly upon those attitudes and behaviours which compromise your integrity. It takes real clarity to see the ways you compress your experience of yourself, restrict your creativity, and diminish your value in your own eyes. As these things become shared they become undone, and the openness that evolves through such sharing has a vitality and truth that strengthens the relationship. In this process lies true intimacy.

THE VALUE OF CONFLICT

There is nothing that cannot be used to deepen your intimacy. Relationship is not meant only to be played out harmoniously in the key of C major; there are sharps, flats, minor keys, and dissonances to enrich the music you make together. An intimate relationship does not fear conflict, but uses it to uncover new depths and to open a deeper sharing. Conflict is not something to avoid, for in its struggles lie the potential for concentrated learning. Conflict is a way-station along the path where differences are fully appreciated and accepted.

Rick and Sally came to one of our weekend workshops with a fear of conflict. Rick was a landscape contractor who also led men's workshops. Sally was a former teacher now raising a family, as well as doing a lot of volunteer work in the school and community. Both were highly articulate, and seemed competent and practical; their very appearance (Rick in ponytail, baseball cap, and work clothes, Sally with straight hair and a long skirt looking every bit the down-to-earth country woman) bespoke a relaxed amiability that put others at ease. Theirs looked to be the picture of a well-functioning marriage, one that included a large circle of friends, a strong presence in the community, and an ability to make things happen for themselves and others.

Nothing we learned about Rick and Sally that weekend contradicted any of these impressions, but during the course of the workshop some other aspects of the picture began to emerge. Their communication revealed a deep dissatisfaction coming from both partners – one that, judging from their tentativeness in talking about it, had rarely been expressed.

For example Rick, after some difficulty in coming up with anything he considered a 'problem' in the relationship (a common

14

difficulty, especially for men), finally launched into something he was careful to label trivial. He said that when he came home frustrated or discouraged by the events of the day, Sally's response would usually give every appearance of sympathy. She would quickly find out what was bothering Rick, question him about it, and take up the problem with gusto. As Rick groused about his difficulties, she would offer all kinds of constructive suggestions. If Rick was having a problem with a guy on his crew, she would have advice on how to deal with it. If he was over-stressed from trying to combine evening job estimates with getting the kids to Little League games, she would offer to arrange car-pooling, or propose rescheduling estimates for the weekend.

On one level, Rick's response to all this was gratitude. How wonderful to have a wife who takes such an interest in your problems and tries to help you solve them. Indeed, Rick admitted, Sally's suggestions were often really good ones. However, on another level, he found himself experiencing deep frustration and resentment. He wasn't sure why. As he spoke, his voice began to rise. Finally it came to him what he really wanted from Sally: 'I wish sometimes you'd just shut up and listen!'

We were all a little surprised by his vehemence, though as he went on it began to make sense. More than anything, Rick wanted Sally to understand how frustrated or angry he felt, before telling him what to do about it.

'How can I even think about what to do when I'm feeling that way?' he asked. 'When you jump in and start trying to fix things it drives me crazy.' Because Rick had never expressed this feeling (partly because he was so ashamed of his own ingratitude), he'd built up quite a charge around the issue. When his resentment erupted, it was with considerable vehemence and anger. Sally was quite taken aback. She had been completely unaware of how this dynamic was affecting Rick. The fact that she was able to hear all this without getting defensive, and show Rick that she understood it, seemed to soften his anger and his face had a new look. 'I never thought I'd be able to tell you this and be heard,' he said. Then he hugged her.

Meanwhile Sally, later in the same session, brought up an issue that had a striking symmetry with Rick's. She had been asked to be head of the board of her local parent-co-operative pre-school, which felt like a great honour. Nevertheless, it was a demanding commitment, and she was not totally sure whether she could take it on, given her other activities. Naturally, she conveyed her dilemma to Rick. He reacted swiftly: 'My God, Sally, you can't be serious. Both of us are already totally stressed out and our finances are stretched. Given that you're at your limit, do you really want to take on a whole new job that pays nothing? Do yourself a favour, tell them to get someone else.'

Even though Rick was ostensibly displaying concern for her well-being, something didn't feel right to Sally. Something in Rick's words, she confessed, had deeply hurt her feelings. As she talked about it in the group, she began to cry. She became aware of a deep sadness and a feeling of worthlessness. As she remained with her feeling, it became clear.

Rather than first acknowledging the rush of pride and pleasure she had felt in being asked to be on the board, Rick had first rushed in with advice, based more on fear than under-standing, carrying a harsh edge to it. Just being asked had meant a great deal to her, had made her feel wanted and accepted by people she cared about. Whether or not she could handle the commitment, she realised, there was a part of her that deeply desired to say yes. By dismissing this entirely, Rick was in effect telling her that none of these feelings mattered. Her joy at being appreciated had been utterly negated by the one person she most wanted to feel appreciated by. 'Weren't you even glad for me?' she asked through her tears. 'Weren't you proud of me? Didn't you understand how much I wanted to do this?'

Rick had no idea how he'd been affecting her. But by the time she was done he found it easy to see the reason for her tears.

In subsequent sessions that weekend Rick and Sally brought up several more of these ostensibly minor issues. As each one came into awareness it was like going through the narrow end of a funnel, into areas of significant disturbance. The couple began to realise how much had remained unspoken over the years and what the price of that silence had been.

Martha and I were struck with how remarkably similar their feelings were. Each wanted more from the other. Each felt the other's behaviour, no matter how seemingly positive, was an obstacle to intimacy. Each craved a degree of closeness that they feared asking for, and each found the lack of intimacy veiled by the superficial harmony of the relationship. In fact the need to maintain peace at all costs was becoming a kind of tyranny. Where there is no room for creative dissonance, no space for partners to share difficult feelings, there is a lack of trust; and where trust is lacking, love cannot fully flourish.

The task Rick and Sally saw for themselves by the end of the workshop was quite different from the one they had pictured at the start. It was not to iron out the few remaining wrinkles in a basically smooth-running partnership. Keeping the surface unruffled was, in fact, what was troubling the depths. Rather the task was to allow dissatisfaction, allow disruption, allow disharmony to occur. In a sense it was to create a larger harmony that had room for disharmony. It meant speaking one's mind when something didn't feel right, and encouraging one's partner to do the same. It meant having the courage to take the risk of not being nice. It was an important revelation for Rick and Sally that all this could be done without shaking the underpinnings of the relationship or impairing their ability to function well together. They came to the workshop feeling like they had to have it together; they left feeling a huge relief that intimacy transcended superficial harmony.

RISK-TAKING AND SAFETY

It will often seem risky to allow unsavoury aspects of yourself to be seen by your partner. Every true intimacy must confront this dilemma. One choice involves taking risks, venturing forth into new and possibly frightening territory, perhaps being honest in potentially painful areas. The other choice is to respect the natural timing for each to learn their lessons by not prematurely forcing things, to create an emotional climate that feels truly safe. A healthy relationship needs to integrate and balance these opposites.

Everyone feels uncomfortable sharing certain personal feelings with their partner. To stay entirely away from these difficult issues leads to an overemphasis on safety and creates an environment so predictable that the relationship becomes dull from want of growth, like Rick and Sally. If you find yourself with an intimacy that has become stale, perhaps you need to take more risks.

On the other hand, if you take too many risks you may have more conflict than the relationship can handle. There is a temptation to disregard the other's vulnerability, which creates a lack of safety. Too much risk-taking subverts the very exploratory climate it means to foster.

Most people have a tendency towards either risk-taking or safety. Those who naturally enjoy risk-taking may sometimes regard their partner, if they are not similarly constituted, as too nice, too careful or even just plain cowardly. Those who lean towards safety may regard the more adventuresome as too pushy, aggressive or insensitive. It is easy to fall into an extreme, to look with disfavour upon the opposite. But it is far more useful to understand the virtue in the opposite, to bring balance into the relationship.

Risk-taking has its virtues, offering excitement and growth. All of us have a tendency to stay within the relatively comfortable limits of our personality, with its known repertoire of feelings and expressions. Limits vary from person to person, and change as we go through life, but we all share the feeling of danger as we approach our personal edge. Risking encourages us to dare and to explore the outer limits of our rage, our tears, our terror, our dark hole. To approach our edge some of us require only a suggestion, while others may need a more concerted and skilful nudging. But for all, its great value lies in the newness it brings into our life.

Safety means security, and this is especially important when feeling vulnerable. When we feel safe we know we won't be attacked or judged, but honoured and respected. Particularly for those of us who are by nature more cautious, this feeling of safety is a crucial ingredient in the willingness to venture beyond the known. Safety balances risk-taking.

Seeking the Treasure

A game is played at children's parties, where the children are searching for a hidden treasure. Someone plays the piano, louder as the children get closer to the treasure, softer as they lose their way.

An intimate relationship consecrated to a spiritual goal has a shared treasure for both parties: the fulfilment of love in its most perfect expression. As partners move together through the ups and downs of daily living, a great piano player offers both encouragement and useful feedback for attaining this treasure.

As the partners open their hearts, when they are more loving and forgiving, the universe plays the music louder, and they feel more alive, happy, fulfilled. When their hearts close, when they are attacking and blaming each other, the universe lets them know they are on the wrong track, also by the way they feel. Their thoughts darken, they become more uncomfortable, have less energy, their bodies lose vitality and health. They have lost their way.

What Could be Simpler?

If both parties are listening carefully to the music, then if one of them gets something in their ear, at least the other one can hear the music clearly. Whoever has the better hearing in the moment can prevail and the leadership can be handed back and forth.

One of the great fruits of this work comes when you experience your partner acting in an unloving way, and watch yourself respond for the first time with compassion instead of hurt or anger. It's a lovely experience, one that feels deeply good to the core. The music has just got a little louder. Such experiences can turn a stuck or dull relationship into one that's passionate, alive, creative.

To listen closely to this music brings an exhilaration into one's life. A new quality is born in the relationship, and one begins to let go of old conditioning that closes the heart. Then all the imperfections can be used as compost to enrich the soil of intimacy. The most difficult times are now seen as blessings in disguise. The alliance has become a sacred vehicle for helping each other come into the fullness of their being.

chapter 2

OPEN-HEARTED LISTENING

What is Being Safe for your Partner?

Nothing is more important to intimacy than a feeling of mutual safety. Have you ever asked yourself what makes you feel safe in a relationship? If you begin to explore this in your daily life, you will probably find that your partner contributes to your feeling of safety in several ways:

> They have room for you to feel whatever you are feeling, and are not threatened by it.

> They are not judging you, or believing they know best what you should be thinking, feeling or doing.

> They honour the path that you have chosen, and wish you well on your journey.

> They care about your existential reality enough to want to understand it fully.

> They let you feel the fullness of their empathy.

When your partner's responses arise from fear, they do not contribute to your feeling of safety. When their responses arise from love, they will help you to feel safe.

Here is one of the greatest challenges in the world of intimacy. We all want to be in the kind of relationship where we could communicate our feelings if we are upset by our partner's behaviour. If this is not possible, a reservoir of frustration and anger builds, and we end up resenting each other. Unfortunately, most intimate relationships are this way.

If you are like most couples, when you express a negative feeling it will usually be perceived by your partner as a threat. Out of their own fear they will typically respond by getting defensive, and you won't be heard. Here are some of the most frequently employed defences:

Putting up an emotional barrier and becoming cold, distant or sullen.

Going on the attack and accusing you of doing something far worse than any of their faults.

Explaining or justifying their behaviour.

Informing you that you are overreacting.

Trying to fix things, preaching how you should regard the situation or what you should do.

Becoming so emotional that they switch the focus from your issue to their feelings.

Dismissing your feelings with humour or sarcasm.

Pretending to listen, saying all the right things, and then proceeding in the same unconscious fashion.

None of these responses brings resolution or facilitates healing, because your partner has closed off to what is really going on for you.

Fortunately there is an alternative response which does bring the desired communication by creating an atmosphere of emotional safety. We call it open-hearted listening. It also could be called emotional yoga.

Just as yoga postures are refined tools that help to open up tight places in the body, this is an equally effective tool for opening up tight places in the heart. The process will quickly reveal where the heart is closed, and show you specifically how to work with it.

This special quality of listening can be used when one of you (or both) is feeling upset, hurt, sad, frustrated, angry, confused, afraid, in short, whenever the feeling of love and peace has departed. The tool is useful if you sense you're about to have an argument or one of you is starting to get defensive. It can be employed when you are not being heard, or if you are going to communicate something which from past experience you feel your partner is unlikely to hear.

WHAT IS LISTENING WITH AN OPEN HEART?

Open-hearted listening replaces defensiveness as a way of responding to our partner's feelings. It allows us to show our partner that are we more interested in understanding their reality than in being right. If we succeed, our partner discovers that not only are we able to see the circumstances through their eyes, but also that we have empathy for their feelings, and can validate them. Great healing results for both parties.

Open-hearted listening is divided into two parts. The first is called mirroring. Our partner begins by telling us some event which has upset them and how they felt about it. We then repeat what they said back to them in our own words. Including as much as we can remember, we give special importance to describing our partner's feelings with accuracy. If their story is getting too long we may always stop them to repeat what they have told up to that point.

It is perfectly natural not to get it right the first time. If we are not exact, or leave something out, our partner lets us know the part that was inaccurate or missing. We reflect back this new part, going back and forth with the process until our partner feels that we have fully reflected the content.

Here is an example of how one couple, Jennifer and Michael, brought greater clarity to their communication through mirroring. Michael was a rural carpenter with a full beard and a pleasant manner. Jennifer, whose work was tending two young children, appeared more highly strung and sensitive.

Michael: We both know that I am dissatisfied with my work and that I want to get a better job, maybe go back to school. I'm not very quick about things. It feels like I'm waiting until the timing feels right to me. Last night you came into the living room when I was relaxing and attacked me about not moving faster. You often criticise me for this and I feel like I'm expected to change overnight. I know I'm not a very motivated person, but I'm working on it. It really annoys me when you nag me like that, especially when I'm down like I was last night. You seem to be saying that you work on your issues and I don't. That makes me feel inadequate.

Jennifer (attempting to mirror): You feel angry because you feel that the way we communicate puts you in the wrong. And you assume, because of my response, that it's your fault.

At this point we told Jennifer that she had changed the meaning on her own behalf when she said 'you assume that', a phrase we discourage in mirroring, because it implies you assume that but I know it really isn't so. In addition, she has left out a great deal. She needed to convey in more detail just what she does to trigger Michael's feelings. She tried again.

Jennifer: When I criticise and blame you for not moving faster at finding new work or going back to school you get

24

angry at me. You want me to know that you are also discontent with the situation, but your rhythms are different to mine. You move more slowly. The way I come on to you makes you feel as though I were saying 'I work on my issues and you don't'. When I do this you feel inferior.

Michael: That was better, but what I said was 'inadequate', not 'inferior'.

Jennifer: When I lambast you for going too slow and imply that I've got it together, you feel inadequate.

Michael: That's right. But you left out the part about your doing it when I am feeling down.

Jennifer: One of the things that makes you feel so inadequate is that I come to you when you are feeling really bad and make it worse by attacking you.

Michael: Yes. You've got it. Oh, and there's one more thing. When you do it I don't feel your love.

Jennifer: In addition to feeling angry at me and feeling inadequate, you also feel that when I come to you this way you don't feel my love.

Michael: I feel well mirrored.

It is not uncommon, after we correctly mirror our partner's original communication, for another level to appear. Being truly heard, often for the first time, can be sufficient to create a new level of safety. Now it may be possible for deeper layers of feelings to emerge. Sometimes the original communication is seen as a piece of a much more expansive concern. The particular incident may reveal unexpected connections to other events, both within the relationship and into the past. In such cases it is good to tell your partner thanks, the mirroring is right, and there is more. Revealing explorations are possible if you are both willing to follow the feelings wherever they lead.

VALIDATION

As important as it is, mirroring is just a prelude. When mirroring is complete, we move on to validation, the place of greatest movement and healing. To validate your partner's feelings is to show them – verbally and non-verbally – that their feelings make sense to you. They are not crazy, exaggerated, or inappropriate. Although they may not be what you would feel, you can imagine a person having such feelings under such circumstances.

It is important to convey that you understand the connection between your actions and their feelings. It is not that your actions caused your partner's feelings, for this would mistakenly absolve them from the part they played. You communicate, rather, that it makes sense to you that, given your role in the exchange, your partner could feel this way.

The quickest way to learn about validation is to have someone actually validate your feelings, and tune into the inner release that follows. It is hard to describe the nature of this experience if you have not undergone it. You will notice a shift in the quality of energy between you. For me, the feeling is, 'Ahh, she finally gets it!' If you don't have this release you may need to tell your partner, 'Sorry, I don't feel validated yet'. Have high standards. When your partner attempts to validate you, check in deeply and honestly with yourself to see if you truly feel validated. It is perfectly acceptable not to feel validated even when you appreciate the sincere efforts of your partner.

Frequently you may feel almost validated, like finding a piece in a jigsaw puzzle that almost fits. Don't settle for almost, because that last bit of work which allows for the piece to fit perfectly is the most important part. See if you can get in touch with what was missing from your partner's attempt and communicate it to them. Maybe you have this feeling because your partner's heart is still a bit closed. Perhaps they were subtly holding on to a feeling of being right, which got transmitted non-verbally and blocked the validation. You might say to your partner on such occasions, 'I could tell you were trying, which I really appreciate; and I still didn't feel fully validated. It felt like you were holding back a little. Is that true?' In this process there is no blame.

This difficulty of holding back, experienced at some point by all who embark on this process, is the most common obstacle to complete validation. The ego proclaims that if I validate your feelings mine are invalid, and that is unacceptable. Therefore my only protection is holding onto being right. This deeply rooted misunderstanding is not always easy to release. Yet validation depends on the disengagement from this false idea, since you will not feel truly validated if I am holding on even a little to the notion that I am right and you are wrong. No matter how skilful my words, you won't experience validation if my heart is closed to you, if I am judging you, if I think you are crazy, or oversensitive, or unworthy for having the feelings you do. If I have such an attitude, I am being asked to go deeper into myself to discover a way of transcending my belief that you shouldn't feel what you do.

What helps me greatly in such a circumstance is to get in touch with something that resembles this situation from my own past experience. If my partner is feeling hurt because I made a decision without consulting her, I attempt to recall if ever there were a case in which I felt similarly upset because I was left out of a decision-making process. If my partner is angry because I failed to keep an agreement, I think back to a time when another's similar lack of integrity triggered my own anger. There is an art to locating such a place within oneself. Sometimes, not being able to find a comparable experience, I can scan my memory for something sufficiently similar, that will allow me to relate to my partner's feelings. If this proves beyond my capacity, imagination may serve, as it did in the following session.

OUT WITH THE BOYS

Paul and Gloria needed to deal with one small problem in an otherwise smooth relationship. Paul, a handsome doctor of fifty, worked and played quite hard. He was an avid golfer, skier, and tennis player. He also enjoyed his time out with men friends, often going to bars for hours after his sporting events, and pouring down quite a few beers. To him this was his natural reward for his focused and highly responsible work.

The problem lay, he felt, with Gloria. He had met her several years ago when she became a nurse at his hospital. They fell madly in love, and Paul left an unhappy marriage to be with Gloria. She was a slim, attractive woman in her early forties who had an air of quiet self-confidence. Although Paul had gone through many relationships, she had given him the gift of his first real intimacy and he still loved her just as much as when they began. However Gloria, who seemed so accepting of Paul's imperfections, was unable to be supportive of his time out with the boys.

Paul wanted to go out with his friends several times a week, with Gloria's blessing. He was trying hard to adapt a reasonable tone. 'Look, you've really been good to me, and also good for me. I know I'm sometimes hard to be around, and you really do a great job putting up with me. So I can't understand why you're making this one thing so difficult for me. There's really no harm in my going out and having a couple of beers with my friends. I work really hard and I deserve to relax. My ex was really uptight about this and used to give me a hard time. I ended up lying to her and then feeling guilty as hell. I really don't want a repeat. I can't understand why you don't just relax and let me have fun. After all, I haven't objected to you hanging out with your women friends. It just doesn't seem fair.'

Gloria listened without interrupting, and when he was finished she seemed uneasy. 'I've never been able to get through to you why I'm so uncomfortable when you go out drinking, but I guess this is the time to do it.' She took a deep breath. 'You know that time last autumn when you had finished playing in the big tournament and I was going to meet you later at the bar?' Paul nodded. 'Well,' she went on, 'I was maybe half an hour late, and when I showed up you had obviously had a few. I could tolerate that, but whenever that waitress in the short skirt came by you reached out to grab her. I was mortified.' 'Aw, come on, you're exaggerating,' Paul replied. 'I was just flirting a little. It's just what men like to do and there's no harm in it. I think you're making a mountain out of a molehill.'

Gloria stood her ground. 'I understand men like to flirt, and I don't mind innocent flirting. I've even been known to do that a bit myself. But what you were doing was stepping over the line. You were totally inappropriate and I was really uncomfortable. In fact, I was downright scared for what this might mean in the future. I picture you going out and drinking and one day you're going to end up in bed with someone.' Paul was beginning to get angry. 'I was not being inappropriate. The trouble with you is you're just too sensitive. There wasn't anything to be afraid of. I'm telling you, it was nothing.' Gloria looked heavenward with an expression that said 'What's the use?' She turned to me. 'This happens every time I try to tell him about how it made me feel. He just doesn't listen.'

After I instructed them in the art of listening, Paul agreed, a bit reluctantly, to hear Gloria. After she spoke he was able to mirror back what she said. However, when it came time to validate her feeling of fear at his behaviour, Paul balked. 'I just don't know how to validate her fear. I can't do it, because I can't relate to it. I really don't understand why she was so upset. Maybe I'm just not cut out for this kind of process.' 'Hang in

· there, Paul,' I answered. 'It's OK that you haven't been able to validate; in fact it's often the case with people who are learning the process. Would you be willing to use your imagination for a moment?' Paul let out an annoyed sigh. 'I guess so.' 'Close your eyes and picture this. You meet up with Gloria at a bar. She's been there for a while before you arrived, and had maybe four or five drinks with her friends. She's dressed in a sexy outfit, exuding her sexuality and enjoying it. A handsome young waiter in very tight pants comes to see if she wants another drink. She looks him over slowly, letting her glance rest on his pelvis. She reaches out and runs her hand languorously down his leg and orders her next drink in a sexy voice. You can tell she would never do this without the alcohol. Now check in for a minute and see how you feel and also how the thought of Gloria going out and drinking with her friends now feels to you.'

Paul kept his eyes closed and paused for a long time. 'OK, I get it.' He looked at Gloria with a slight smile and took her hands. 'Gloria, I understand now why you felt fear at the way I was flirting in the bar. I can see why you'd think, if I was coming on so strong on this one occasion, that it might lead somewhere if you weren't there and I'd had a few more drinks under my belt. When I pictured you doing the same thing it didn't feel very good at all. I get it.'

Gloria was validated. Of course, the issue of her supporting Paul in going out with his friends had not been resolved; but any further discussion on the matter would now take place at an entirely different level of understanding.

When the need to be right is replaced by the desire to understand, it is usually possible to find some way of getting inside your partner's feelings. There may be a temptation to assume that your partner's experience is simply too different from anything in your own past for you to grasp. Before you succumb, consider that our similarities outweigh our differences. All have experienced the basic human feelings of hurt, sadness, fear, frustration, or anger. In the act of finding some feeling in you that resembles your partner's upset, you may be graced with a valuable insight or a moment of opening.

This does not in any way mean that you must agree with your partner's assessment of the situation. It does not mean that you have to make yourself wrong or guilty for your feelings. It does not mean your partner is good and you are bad, or that you have to change your behaviour or give up anything. It often does, however, bring you a more enlightened perspective on some of your unconscious behaviour patterns, at which you might then wish to take a closer look.

An example might help. You have two children who are having a difficult time with each other. The older wants to spend some time alone with a visiting friend. She finds her younger brother's unwanted intrusion a nuisance and tells him to leave her alone. The brother feels hurt from being left out, and keeps trying to include himself, only to be forcefully rebuffed. They come to you, each upset and blaming their sibling. To create a safe environment for each one does not involve making the other wrong, or denying their feelings. They are both right. The older child deserves freedom from intrusion, while the younger's pain at exclusion is perfectly understandable. It is easy to validate the feelings of both. This is the spirit to keep in your heart as you are exploring what it means to validate your partner. Both your feelings are valid, and yours are temporarily on hold.

HINTS FOR SUCCESSFUL VALIDATION

It is natural at first to experience some obstacles on the way to successful validation. Your validation will improve with practice. As you are learning to work things through with your partner, it helps to keep in mind several key points.

Be specific. Instead of, 'I can see how you didn't like it when I did that', say, 'I can understand your feeling of hurt and abandonment when I made another appointment after agreeing to spend Saturday afternoon with you'.

Be direct. Instead of, 'When you feel ignored by me ... ' try 'When I turn away from you ... ' The key is to be direct, specific, and simple.

Be precise. There is a distinction between 'I understand that you feel angry when I keep interrupting you', and 'I understand how my continual interruptions would make you angry'. The first, 'I understand that ... ' does not convey a true sense of comprehending your partner's reality. It is more mirroring than validation. The second statement conveys a true validation.

Be attentive to the non-verbal message. Be conscious about how close you sit (many couples err on the side of sitting too far away from each other; but check the distance out with your partner to make sure you are both comfortable with it). Consider if holding hands feel right. Face each other and make eye contact. Be especially aware of the message conveyed in your tone of voice, as well as in the look in your eyes, or your body language. Observe how crossed arms convey a message of defensiveness. Have you let go of being right?

Be aware of your partner's feelings and level of intensity. Sometimes you may get the feeling right, but not understand just how intense it was for your mate. It is hard to convey an understanding of a fervent feeling with a casual tone.

Be persistent. Many situations require a number of attempts before the validation is successful. Don't let seeming failure get you down; the last arduous 5% is worth the struggle, and has within it the potential for learning of great depth.

Of course, it is the nature of this process that you, too, will have a chance to be validated. Both partners have equal responsibility to listen with an open heart. In actual practice, if your partner feels heard and validated, they will be far more motivated to make whatever effort is needed to do the same for you. It is especially true here that you get back what you put out.

What if I'm being Unfairly Attacked?

Many have wondered whether they have an obligation to continue open-hearted listening if they perceive their partner is using it repeatedly to attack them unfairly.

Willy and Julia had learned open-hearted listening at one of our workshops. Julia, a strong and attractive woman of 50, seemed quite in touch with her feelings and willing to express them. Willy, a few years older, had abandoned a promising career as an Ivy-League intellectual in order to live close to the land in Vermont. He gave the impression of much going on under the surface.

Immediately after the workshop they had practised a great deal with listening to each other and seemed to be doing well. But one day they showed up in distress, because they had been going around in circles on the same issue for some time. Julia began, 'I feel absolutely exasperated! When I ask you to listen with an open heart, you agree, but then close down and refuse to continue the minute I express any kind of negative feeling. I can't say anything to you!' Willy took offence. 'That's not fair. You know I'm perfectly willing to listen as long as you're not indulging it as an excuse to give out to me. I'm happy to listen to your feelings; but you don't just tell me how you're feeling. You blame me, assault me, and make me into a villain. There's nothing in the rules that says I have to just sit there and take that kind of abuse.'

Julia appeared extremely frustrated. 'Look, I know that I sometimes lose my temper, and there have been occasional times where I attacked you. But I've been really working hard for quite a while at trying to communicate more cleanly and without blame.' Her anger became mixed with tears, as she cried out, 'You never acknowledge me for all the work that I've done! I don't always come at you with attack and blame. I honestly think that most of the time I'm just stating how I feel. But if I show a hint of emotion you close right down and claim that I haven't presented it right, for God's sake! I have to be some kind of perfect saint, without any negative feelings, for you to even deign to listen.' 'You're still not being fair,' Willy retorted. 'You may think that you come across objective and clean, but I wish you could see a tape of yourself. Then you'd see how much you're attacking me. If you were really as fair as you claim to be I wouldn't have any problem listening.' He turned towards me and pleaded, 'I shouldn't have to put up with verbal abuse in doing this, should I?' Julia, with tears in her eyes, responded, 'Do I have to have my act totally together for him to listen? Don't I get a certain amount of latitude in my feelings? Isn't the whole point of this that you hear your partner even when they are upset? Even very upset?'

This is a complex issue. On the one hand you want to create an environment where all feelings are permissible, where it's acceptable to be human. The listener mustn't hold up exalted standards of emotional purity for their partner to express themselves and be heard. (At this point Julia nodded vigorously with a slight smile on her face, while Willy looked glum.)

On the other hand, there are people who misuse openhearted listening. Having a captive audience, they dump their negativity on their partner in an unfair manner. (Now it was Willy's turn to smile, while Julia expression became suddenly more brittle).

Neither Willy nor Julia was wrong, although there was work to be done. Intimacy requires that you learn to stretch in two directions. First, you discover how to be present for all of your partner's feelings without regard to how fair they seem to be. It is difficult to listen when you think you are being unfairly assaulted, but it is well worth learning the art of non-defensiveness. Your partner's negative feelings can be seen as outpourings of a hurt child rather than as evidence of your inadequacy. Let go of the need to make sense of your partner's emotions. (*See chapters 7 and 11*)

However, while learning to be fully present for your partner's feelings you are also discovering the importance of taking responsibility for the way you express your own emotions.

In having your partner listen, watch yourself carefully for the assumption that they are responsible for causing your negative feelings. If you harbour such a belief, you are likely to look without compassion at your partner's imperfections, and to expend a fair amount of energy blaming them for not being sufficiently loving or supportive. You have a critical role in the creation of your own emotional state.

Many of us expect the impossible from our partner. Not having received the wise, mature love we needed as children, we expect our partner to do for us what our parents couldn't, to fill our emptiness by always being loving, supportive, or positive, and always in touch with our feelings. We have forgotten that the only place we can find the unconditional love that will heal us is from the source within.

On top of such unrealistic demands, we can become enamoured of open-hearted listening and make it a tool of our confusion. Now that our partner is finally listening without defense, it is tempting to begin unloading our backlog of negative feelings! Instead of bringing understanding and compassion, an originally loving tool can result in greater separation, blame, and conflict. In such an atmosphere our partner will soon come to associate open-hearted listening with being continually abused, and will inevitably find grounds to avoid doing it. If things aren't going well, ask yourself these questions:

Is it a two-way communication? When one party dominates by doing most of the asking, something has gone off balance and needs correction. To receive the full benefit both parties need to experience the process in both directions.

Are you doing it too often? We have grounds for caution if we employ open-hearted listening continually to point out to our partner the ways they fall short of our lofty standards. Space is needed to acknowledge each other's virtues and to enjoy life together without endless processing.

Are both parties taking responsibility for their negative feelings? Instead of, 'You're always scaring the hell out of me with those childish outbursts of yours', try instead, 'When you lose your temper that way I feel afraid'. If we find ourselves more often assuming the role of the injured, innocent victim than questioning the significance of our own role, perhaps fear has taken hold of a loving tool and has begun to misuse it.

COMMITMENT TO LISTEN

Open-hearted listening is fully effective only when you have a commitment to do it any time it is requested (or as soon afterwards as is practically possible). Without such a commitment you will be embarking on a half-hearted journey, severely limiting yourselves by backing away from the very moments that most require your dedicated courage and attention.

Commitments have no meaning when things come easy. If your life unfolded without challenge or obstacle, you would need no commitment. Commitment helps you respond with a deeper purpose during difficult times, such as when your partner is engaged in unloving behaviours or moods. Commitment is a discipline in the face of what your fear would like to do when faced with a difficult situation. It is your ally against the temptation to take the easy road, to

indulge in the immediate gratification of being right and closing your heart. The more difficult the temptation, the stronger
your commitment needs to be.

Fasting has taught me much about responding to temptation. Whenever I decide to fast, I always get ravenously hungry
at some point, especially in the first couple of days. On many
occasions I am able to say no to my craving, stay on track and
continue the fast. Sometimes, the first time I get really hungry I
give in, rationalising to myself that this was not really the right
time to fast. The difference between the two situations is that in
the first case, whether I knew it or not, I had the natural discipline that arises out of a true commitment. Successful fasting
entails taking into account the strength of the hunger you will
likely feel and greeting it with a resolve of equal power.

In order to accomplish any goal you have to take fully into
account the strength of the force that resists it, a force which the
Russian spiritual teacher, G. Gurdjieff, called 'second force'.
When you commit to open-hearted listening it is necessary to
acknowledge the power of second force, the profound temptation to get defensive when your partner's annoying behaviour
elicits your strong negative reaction. Your partner will accuse
you unfairly, or look at you in a certain way, or employ a certain
tone, and every ounce of your being will crave to attack them or
defend yourself, or just give up. You will be tempted time and
again, when they are expressing their hurt and fear, to pull back
or attack. Fear will assert that you can't be present and open for
your partner. Only the strength of your commitment will help
you meet and overcome second force.

If your child, or someone you deeply care for, got severely
ill, and you had to climb a mountain at night in the rain to get
the only available medicine, would you not find the energy to
do it? There is no question in your mind, it does not even occur
to you not to, even if you are tired, sick, or not in the mood.
When you make a strong commitment from your heart you
have aligned yourself with something deeper than your own

personal needs. A strength and power are available far beyond what the limited mind thinks possible.

Sometimes the struggle can be extremely wearisome. At moments you need to go within and reach for a place that you did not even know existed. Commitment reminds you that it is worth the effort to take the more difficult path. The more resistance you have the more likely you will learn something of inestimable value by struggling with your deeply-rooted tendency to close down. For those warriors who embark on this path your rewards will be beyond anything you could imagine.

DOES LISTENING WITH AN OPEN HEART ELIMINATE USEFUL DIALOGUE?

Some people experience a reluctance to communicate one way at a time, fearing this inhibits useful dialogue. Of course real dialogue is indispensable. But the quality of communication is limited when one or both parties are not truly heard. If dialogue is attempted without this understanding, it is likely to result in mutual blame and a great expenditure of energy in a futile attempt to be understood.

Greg and Tanya came to one of our couples weekends, stuck in a conflict about his single incidence of infidelity many years ago. Greg had been contrite, acknowledging that it was a serious mistake and promising never to repeat it. Nevertheless, Tanya was unable to forgive him. She was convinced that Greg had not fully understood the depth of her feeling of betrayal. Whenever a major fight erupted, Tanya would bring up his infidelity and attack him with it. Greg would defend himself, saying, 'Look, how many times can I apologise? The past is over. Why can't we just let it go and start living in the present?'

Whenever this issue got brought up there was an unsatisfying feeling to the dialogue. Greg felt unfairly attacked for something which was past and gone, something for which he had apologised. Tanya felt frustrated at not being able to release powerful feelings which had never been fully heard.

Two errors are common when past mistakes cast their shadow over the present. Tanya would be tempted by the first – to attack one's partner for their mistake, enjoying the feeling of being the righteous, wounded party. Greg would find it enticing to make the second mistake, desiring prematurely to let go of the the past and move on, overlooking the importance of having patience with painful, unresolved old wounds. In truth, the past is neither to be indulged nor dismissed, but to be learned from.

What was to be done? After we showed them how to listen with an open heart, Tanya asked Greg to do so while she explored the depth of her feelings. It was hard for Greg not to be defensive, but he made a supreme effort to listen and validate, for which Tanya acknowledged him. It helped Tanya to remember that while her partner had made a dramatic mistake, he was not a bad person.

She did not feel complete enough on this one occasion to release her feelings totally. But because she appreciated Greg's new effort to enter into her feelings, Tanya agreed to avoid using the incident to attack him. Greg acknowledged that her feelings were valid for as long as she needed to have them. They both agreed that it would be valuable to explore the feelings further at a later time, but to wait a while until the trust level improved through listening around other issues.

To justify and enjoy negative feelings is indeed a temptation. But Tanya realised that the pleasure of dwelling permanently in the role of innocent victim was not worth the cost. Her willingness to forgive was the key, even though she had not yet been able to release her feelings of anger and blame. With the help of Greg's new capacity to hear and validate, Tanya was able over time to forgive her partner completely.

DOES OPEN-HEARTED LISTENING DESTROY FREEDOM?

There are those who, on hearing of open-hearted listening, conclude that it would destroy freedom and spontaneity in the relationship.

Some hold the strange notion that freedom means doing what they want in the moment. For example, if I make a commitment to exercise every day for the next week, this logic suggests that by forcing myself to exercise, I'm sacrificing my freedom and spontaneity. I wish to retain the 'freedom' to follow the whims of my cravings, my addictions and my desire for immediate gratification. But being a slave to my cravings, whether they be for drugs, laziness, or indulging my ego, could scarcely be called freedom. This kind of freedom is actually the freedom of a machine, a spontaneity based on limited conditioning or addictions.

To break my old physical or mental reactive patterns, I create disciplines. These structures seem to be limiting spontaneity, since they are often conceived as forcing oneself to do what one would rather avoid. But discipline is what arises naturally when I allow my behaviour to be determined by my deeper wisdom rather than by my desire for immediate gratification. In order to have true spontaneity it is necessary first to interrupt the old reactive behaviour. Discipline opens the door to real freedom, since I am no longer in reaction.

Just as a commitment to exercise replaces a sedentary lifestyle, a discipline such as open-hearted listening breaks the old habit of responding in a mechanical fashion to my partner.

'BUT WILL THEIR BEHAVIOUR CHANGE?'

We are often told that open-hearted listening sounds very good in theory but has no value if your partner validates your feeling about their unwanted behaviour and then keeps doing the same thing.

Although there can be no guarantees, we can offer encouragement to those with this concern. Martha and I found that as we listened to each other hundreds of times over the years, we became more finely tuned to each other's reality. As time went on we started catching ourselves on the point of behaving unskillfully towards each other more often. We perceived connections between seemingly unrelated events, as unconscious patterns began to reveal themselves. It was neither our partner's complaints nor demands that led to alterations in our behaviour, but rather our greater awareness of ourselves.

Change takes time. Deeply ingrained behavioural patterns are not so easy to alter. If you are in the habit, for example, of speaking to your partner with a sharp edge to your voice whenever they do something that does not work for you, watch how easy it is to fall into that unconscious pattern, even if you say to yourself that you would like to break the habit. Remember, it is just as difficult for your partner to overcome their own long-term patterns of unconscious behaviour as it is for you.

Even if negative behaviour persists for a while, you may notice your partner sometimes remembering. Be gracious when your partner forgets, encourage them lovingly when they succeed. If a problem persists, at least you have created an environment more conducive to a creative solution. Your faith in your partner's capacity to change will help them become more conscious of their actions.

A DAY OF GRACE: ANOTHER LEVEL OF COMMITMENT

Here is a powerful structure for couples who wish to accelerate their growth and learn a great deal about themselves in a short time.

If you have seen the value of releasing your usual defences in listening with an open heart, the next step extends this gift of love for a whole day. You will know if and when the time has come to try.

The structure takes place in a two-day period and consists of a commitment by one person to keep their heart open to their

41

partner for the entire day. The following day their partner does the same. The commitment holds no matter what your partner says or does. You will not attack your partner in any way, for any reason, nor may you be defensive. You will be constantly alert for creative new ways to express your love.

You do not have to do everything they wish, or accept outrageous behaviour. A parent can be loving towards a child even while setting firm boundaries. When a child is most wounded, love is most needed.

You are being asked to play the part of a person with a perfectly open heart. This happened to an unknown Italian actor, who played the role of Jesus in a major production about his life. After the filming, the actor's whole life was profoundly altered. Even playing the part of a person with a perfectly open heart can apparently have a remarkably healing effect! For an entire day you put aside all fear-based behaviour and behave to your partner as if you did not have an ego.

Your partner can revel for a day in something they have probably never experienced in their whole life (unless they had a parent capable of mature love). They can relax and be who they are, knowing they will not be judged or blamed.

If you fail to keep your heart open, do not make excuses. Simply stop and do whatever is necessary to connect once again with your heart, to restore yourself once again to a place of non-judgement. You are not asked to be perfect, but you are asked not to make excuses. Do whatever it takes to honour your commitment, although it may sometimes feel profoundly difficult.

If your partner is being difficult and you feel that it's impossible to be loving, do not give in. If you have the intention, the universe will lean in your direction and meet you with the help you need. Although keeping this commitment can sometimes be emotionally strenuous, it is also an opportunity for immense growth.

As this process increases the feeling of safety in your relationship, deeper levels of pain may emerge for the first time in your life. Since nothing can be released until it is first made conscious, your wounds can now at last be healed. At times you might both temporarily wish you had chosen a path of less intensity. But there is a joy in doing this work, for you are not only healing yourselves, you are also helping to heal the whole split between men and women.

A wonderful variation is to give your partner a Day of Grace without telling them you are doing so. A special pleasure arises from the purity of such a gift.

THE IMPORTANCE OF DOING IT BOTH WAYS

Both roles in the Day of Grace are profoundly valuable. For me, just to be able to have the full permission to be who I am in safety has significantly increased my level of trust. I have come to know that Martha will be there for me no matter how unsavoury my moods. The fact that I have felt so unconditionally accepted has helped me safely release many emotional toxins, and to make greater peace with my own imperfections.

Were I to be either the wounded one or the safe one all the time, there would be an imbalance. But the value lies in playing the roles of both the wounded and the healer in succession, which shakes me loose from my conditioning more powerfully than either role possibly could by itself.

When we first started I looked forward to the days when Martha would play the role of healer. But I soon found, if anything, the days I was healer were even more enjoyable and beneficial. In helping to heal Martha, I was healing something similar in myself.

When I made a decision at the beginning of the day to keep my heart open, I encountered numerous occasions when I was about to react negatively to what Martha said or did. These became opportunities to allow in another dimension of awareness, and to make a different choice.

As time went on I began to find new and more creative ways of expressing my love during these special days. For example, in communicating about some practical matter, such as the need to pay the bills, it's possible to speak without attack in a perfectly neutral fashion. But it's also possible to say the same thing with the heart engaged. I began to be interested in the tone of voice that I used for the most mundane communications. It was so much more possible than I had imagined to express my love in a variety of subtle ways. The opportunities for greater love and awareness in daily interaction were unlimited! What had started as an exercise developed a life of its own, which took us far beyond any structure.

The Day of Grace is a blessing of the highest order. It has shown me how to let go of my belief that I am a victim of my partner's moods. No matter what the content, I always have the option of choosing love, which is more powerful than fear.

chapter 3

ASKING YOUR PARTNER
FOR CHANGE

THE USUAL RESPONSES DON'T WORK

How many of us have had the following experience? You tell your partner there's something they do on a regular basis that really bothers you. And they reply, 'Oh yes, I can see I've really been unconscious. I understand how that would bother you and of course I'll be glad to change. If I forget, please remind me'. Chances are, it's not very often.

Some of the most powerful difficulties in being a couple stem from our frustrations with our partner's behaviour. No one after the initial romantic stage can avoid being annoyed or frustrated by some of their partner's habits. In a healthy relationship we should be able to communicate about such disturbances, ask our partner respectfully to alter the offending behaviour, and expect that they would at least listen carefully and take our request seriously.

45

The reality is generally otherwise. More likely, you respond to your partner's undesirable behaviour like this:

You attack. 'You're always such a total slob! What's the matter with you, didn't you ever learn basic manners? Why the hell don't you clean up after yourself?' In response to such attack your partner is likely to resent you for not accepting them in their more casual relationship to order. Even if they do honour the request for change, they still resent you for the highly disrespectful way you asked. If they do not honour it, there are bad feelings on both sides.

You resign and resent. After fruitless attempts to get your partner to change, you resign yourself to the fact that they will never change. In so doing you bury your negative feelings and end up resenting your partner. Resignation, while it may superficially resemble acceptance, is quite far removed from the feeling of peace that accompanies true acceptance.

You manipulate. Your style is more indirect, so you use subtle means to try controlling your partner's behaviour. When people accuse you of manipulation, what they usually mean is that they do not like the undercover methods with which you are trying to influence them. Nothing is wrong with trying to affect your partner's behaviour. It feels a lot better to both parties, however, when you do so awarely. Instead of making manipulation into a sin, learn to be conscious and above board about the ways you influence each other.

None of these addresses the real issue or elicits a lasting change. It does work if you become allies with your partner to be more conscious, without blame, about what does not feel good together. It is challenging to deal wisely with annoying habits that cast a shadow on your harmony.

CONTROL AND SURRENDER

If I am using my relationship in my spiritual growth, how do I justify asking my partner to change their behaviour? Doesn't this go against the common spiritual dictate that says I should accept my partner just as they are?

You need both to communicate effectively about what bothers you and to accept your partner's imperfections with grace. If the first is missing you become a martyr with growing resentments; if the second is missing you become a sophisticated nag who can be very annoying to be around. The first represents control; the second, surrender. For a harmonious intimacy, control and surrender must be purified of their fearful aspects.

Fearful control emerges as an authoritative and bossy style. Your manner conveys that your partner had better do as you wish or you will make their life miserable. Those caught up in fearful control will try frequently to take charge of their partner's behaviour in order to lessen their own feeling of fear or inadequacy.

Fearful surrender displays itself as weak, placating and submissive. You put out the message that you are powerless and your partner may do whatever they wish with you. Whoever is caught up in this state will invite and allow themselves to be controlled unhealthily. Destructive control and surrender often attract each other. Although they may seem like opposites, they are actually opposing sides of the same coin. Neither is a whole response or a genuine acknowledgement of your love.

However, control and surrender can have an entirely different flavour when they arise from a place of respect for both yourself and your partner.

Healthy control is neither bullying nor manipulative. Rather, it represents the male force elevated to its highest potential. It arises out of the realisation that you are not a victim of the world you see, that you have the choice to alter your consciousness and master your circumstances. It is a recognition of the ways that you contribute, outwardly and inwardly, to whatever feels out of tune with the highest good, and a willingness to say NO! to these harmful patterns. Healthy control may manifest as self-discipline, taking charge of your attitude, diet, exercise, or habits.

Healthy control can also display itself as saying no to your partner. For example, in becoming clear about your boundaries, you may respectfully ask your partner to change some of their unconscious behaviour that is not healthy for the relationship.

Healthy surrender is not submission, nor is it self-abnegation. Rather, it is the feminine aspect elevated to its highest potential. To surrender is to cease resisting, to be less brittle, more receptive and penetrable. If you do not like what is happening, take that as a cue to relax. Like water, continually shifting its shape, blend with what is happening. Healthy surrender manifests both as loving acceptance of your own imperfections and a willingness to allow your partner to be who they are, including those traits you may not find too attractive.

WHO IS RESPONSIBLE FOR MY FEELINGS?

When I ask my partner for a change, am I implying that their behaviour is the source of my bad feelings? After all, am I not responsible for the way I feel? Anyone with much exposure to new age thinking will be tempted instantly to answer that they are. In today's more sophisticated spirituality, it has become a virtual cliché.

But it doesn't seem at all obvious that I am responsible for my feelings. Almost all of us share the common belief that if you criticise me in an unkind manner and immediately I feel bad, it's your fault for causing me to feel that way. It pays to assess with honesty if, perhaps, underneath my spiritually proper belief structure, I still believe that my partner is the source of my unhappiness.

One way of telling is by watching the extent to which I blame my partner for the way I feel. Can I believe I am responsible for my feelings and simultaneously blame my partner for the way I feel? Obviously not. But if I am responsible for my feelings, is there appropriate justification for asking my partner to change behaviour which is annoying me?

We think so. It's possible to take responsibility for my feelings and still reasonably ask my partner to change their behaviour. But it is important to be aware of my motivation.

WHEN FEAR ASKS FOR CHANGE

When you ask for a change of behaviour, your request can arise out of fear or love. For example, if you are a person who deals with insecurity by having your holiday planned out to the last detail when your partner acts on vacation more from impulse, you may well become frustrated or annoyed with them. If you request that they be more like you, planned and organised, they may feel you are rigid and constricted. Your fear is asking them to change.

Whenever you blame your partner for your uncomfortable emotional state, you are indulging in an ego-based request for change. Your request will likely come through with the message that there is something wrong with them. Your partner will feel judged and in all likelihood not want to honour the request. They may well feel that you are trying unfairly to control them, or to deny some essential aspect of their being. Not wanting to honour your request will have a truth to it.

For example, Frank tells Lynn it really worries him when she goes off climbing mountains. He asks her to stop such dangerous activity and find a safer form of recreation. Since this request is fear-based, it will have a quality that doesn't feel right to Lynn. For her, climbing is an indispensable expression of who she is, and she probably won't find herself interested in honouring the request. She might, however, explore Frank's fear with him, and ask him, if there is any way, short of giving up something that really nourishes her, that she can help him deal with his fear.

Say you and your partner come from widely divergent backgrounds. She might come from a family that emphasised privacy over intimacy, while your family shared everything together at the expense of privacy. In such a case she might be uncomfortable with your style of intimacy, which she perceives as not respecting her boundaries. And you might equally be uncomfortable with her style, perceiving it as withholding.

If she asks you to change, she may be failing to see that your way of relating, although very different in style from hers, is as valid as her own. Again, these are not healthy grounds for you to want to change. However, the knowledge of each other's past may certainly bring a new awareness and a greater respect for the other.

Or perhaps a man might ask a woman to be more rational, to stop allowing herself to be so led by her feelings. He is essentially echoing the popular song, 'Why can't a woman be more like a man?' This was well expressed in a cartoon we both liked, showing a dog and a cat lying in bed together, both looking sullen. The cat is saying, 'Look, I'm not aloof, it's just I'm a cat, OK?' Asking partners to alter something essential in their nature just brings more conflict.

Sometimes the way a request is initially framed may stimulate in your partner a fear that if they said yes they would have to give up something important. A woman is frightened by the intensity of her partner's anger, and asks him please not to get angry at her. While he may have had some learning to do about expressing his anger more wisely, he likely feels there is something fundamentally unfair about his partner's request. And there is. To ask your partner not to have their feelings is tantamount to asking them to abandon their humanity.

The woman, however, might let her partner know that he needed to be able to get angry, and she needed to be able to feel safe. Then she might ask if he were willing to work together to find a way of dealing with anger that feels safe to her. With such a request her partner is not being asked to give up anything essential.

WHEN LOVE ASKS FOR CHANGE

Request for change can have different motives. In a spiritual relationship one of our functions is to serve each other in a unique role as a teacher, since there are many discordant areas of our being about which our partner has unique knowledge.

It's as if, in learning a martial art, you have a teacher who sees that you aren't putting your full effort into a move. The teacher coaxes you lovingly. 'Come on, I know you can do better than that. Put your whole attention into that movement.' Such a teacher serves you by not accepting anything less than your best. In fact, that is precisely why you have employed him, to help you be more conscious.

It is possible to look similarly upon your partner as someone with whom you have contracted to help each other live more consciously. You are offering each other the invitation to look more closely at the very things you have come into this world to heal in yourself. Whether in a direct request or by an innate understanding, you ask your partner to tell you when they sense that your behaviour might not be in alignment with your deepest purpose. If your candle flickers you ask them to please share their light with you, and pledge to do the same for them.

In our relationship, Martha's requests for a change in my behaviour have often revolved around my failure to pick up after myself. If our life together were a musical composition, such behaviour would be a note or passage that was out of tune. The first signal of my out-of-tune behaviour may lie in Martha's discomfort. It can be an act of love for her to ask that I play more in tune. I still sometimes cringe at being reminded of my shortcomings, but underneath I sense that what my partner is asking of me would be a gift to me were I to do it. If I don't feel the value for myself in my partner's request, then even if I follow it I'm going to do so resentfully and it's not going to feel right.

Your partner will serve as your spiritual teacher if you have the ears to hear and are willing to abandon defence. Having lived with you and experienced the consequences of your habits and tendencies, they are likely to be acutely aware of those areas where you are most out of touch. Of course it is well that they point out imperfections lovingly rather than conveying, 'Oh God, there you go again!' When you feel more accepted you are less likely to get defended and push away the truth of what is being said. Your partner can serve as the voice of your deeper self, come to ask you to examine an aspect of your life which could be more in harmony.

Have Faith in Your Partner

I once performed with a second-rate symphony orchestra. We were playing a piece with a big solo for the French horn section, who frequently hit the wrong notes. The conductor, an imposing and dignified man, had come to conduct the dress rehearsal and concert. During their solo the horns again hit a few wrong notes. The regular conductor had come to expect this and had got used to it. But the guest conductor stopped them short and asked them to repeat. When again a few notes were missed, he brought everything to a dead halt and looked at them piercingly. 'That simply won't do!' he intoned in a manner which I have never forgotten. That was all he said. The horns got it right and did so at the concert. They succeeded because the distinguished conductor had believed they were capable.

You can contribute to the success of your partner in changing unwanted behaviour by believing in their capacity to change. Studies repeatedly show that students who have difficulties continue to do poorly when their teachers have little faith in them. These same students, working with teachers who believe in them, perform surprisingly well.

Of course there is the temptation to dismiss your partner as one who has proven repeatedly that they can't change. Many send their partners the message, 'You have never changed and never will'. Your conscious and unconscious attitude about your partner's capacity to change sends them a message they take seriously. It often becomes a self-fulfilling prophecy. It is worth cultivating the perspective that your partner, despite past failures, is quite capable of moving together with you towards greater awareness.

COMMON DESTRUCTIVE PATTERNS

Certain forms of unconscious behaviour are quite prevalent. If you recognise any of the following in your relationship, they might serve as a useful starting place to practice asking for a change in behaviour.

Discouragement. One partner will make a suggestion or share a dream for the future, and the other will instantly find flaws or objections. This will soon discourage the first one from sharing their ideas. Brainstorming sessions in a business meeting can be a model for a different kind of response. All ideas are initially welcomed and only later are they culled. Become allies in creating an atmosphere of emotional safety when one of you shares an idea or a vision.

Correction. How many times have we witnessed someone telling a story only to be annoyingly corrected by their partner with some irrelevancy? A flow is interrupted for no good reason. Once Martha was expressing how impressed she was that our son got to go up in both a balloon and a helicopter within a month. I immediately informed her that it was not a month, it was six weeks. Her enthusiasm was effectively punctured and there was no place to go with it. In addition, my correction had served no useful purpose. Fortunately, she caught what had happened and used it to frame a request to me that I be more conscious of my motives should I feel the need to correct her. Since then I have noticed how often the urge to provide 'greater accuracy' has no redeeming social value. One more occasion to put into practice the truth that there are many things better left unsaid.

Interruption. In some subcultures, such as the one I grew up in around New York City, it is considered all right to interrupt. In other cultures it is considered the height of rudeness. The person being interrupted may often feel as if their partner has no interest in what is being said and can't wait to speak their own, more worthwhile piece. If you do not appreciate being interrupted, here is an opportunity to let the interrupter know that you are bothered, without blaming them. And should they forget and interrupt, avoid responding either by getting angry or putting up with it. Instead, try simply saying in a pleasant tone, 'Just a second, wait until I'm finished'.

A DIFFICULT REQUEST

My wife Martha, by virtue first of being so close to me, perceives many unaware aspects of my behaviour. As a woman, she can see clearly in some directions where men tend to be less insightful. I have learned to develop a great respect for her perceptions of my behaviour. When she asks me for a behaviour change it usually has a power and a rightness to it. I have learned not to dismiss her observations too glibly. I may safely assume a high probability that there is something for me to look at in her requests.

In particular I recall one request that was very hard for me to hear. Among my male friends we have an easy and direct way of putting forth our personal needs, assuming that our friends will do likewise, working things out without conflict. As a result I had a habit with Martha of communicating my wishes forcefully, and assuming that if she had a contrary desire she would make it known, after which we could negotiate.

It did not work out that way. Martha felt that I too often prevailed with my more dominant manner, seeming to lack interest in her possibly different wishes. Many women have this experience with their men.

I would put out quite unequivocally that I wanted to go to the hot springs over the holidays, because I felt the need for some deep relaxation. As a woman, Martha didn't find it so easy to break in and let me know she had a real yearning for the mountains, and that we needed to negotiate. Instead she would build resentment, because I seemed to be putting out my needs so strongly that they brooked no contradiction.

After many failed attempts to understand, I finally realised that she was not asking me to do whatever she wanted, to sacrifice the strength of my feelings. I learned after much struggle to make a seemingly minor, but important, change: after declaring that I had a really strong urge to go to the hot springs, I asked her, 'And what would you like to do?' Such a simple addition! Yet it made all the difference to Martha, who felt at last that she didn't have to yell to be heard.

If you take an inner snapshot whenever one of you does something that bothers the other, you may perceive a pattern that connects the various incidents. For example, one major theme might occur when your partner is feeling hurt or angry. Perhaps you would like for them to be conscious of their feelings, articulate them without blame, and communicate what they want from you, rather than just withdrawing or criticising. We find that a great many couples struggle with this issue.

A CENTRAL REQUEST

A few years ago Martha and I were going through some rapids in our stream. We were quarrelling more often than I felt comfortable with. Something was nagging at me for a long time, but I couldn't quite put my finger on it.

One day when we had just completed a run together on a rustic Vermont dirt road, I realised there was something essential I had been wanting from Martha without having articulated it. I suspect that most intimacies contain a quintessential unstated request, something fundamental that we want from our partner and haven't asked in a clear, direct way.

I had been noticing conflict between us whenever I would get into one of my deep, dark Russian Jewish moods. I sensed Martha's fear and discomfort with me at such times, and her interest in getting me quickly out of my state so she could feel at ease once again. It felt as though she had doubts as to whether I would ever emerge from this darkness. I noticed she would either try to make things better or get short with me. Sometimes it was rather subtle. But I hadn't been feeling the sense of safety that comes when my partner accepts me.

I had never been clear enough about this to ask it of Martha directly. But now, on this sparkling autumn day in Vermont, I asked her if she would hear a really fundamental request.

'I want you to honour and respect my rhythms and see the positive contribution my darkness brings into my life. Please stop treating my darkness as a disease to be cured. I want to know it is deeply OK with you that I go as fully as needed into my darkness. I want your support in getting to the very bottom. I want you to have faith in my process and in me. Please hear me, I want this with my whole being.'

Martha was able to hear me and responded favourably. She promised to be there for me as I went into my depths. And she has. Not surprisingly, in feeling her support, I have found myself needing to enter into darkness less often.

WHEN EGO CONTAMINATES A TRUE MESSAGE

A common difficulty with many couples is the intrusion of blame into an otherwise legitimate message. Sometimes your partner's message originates from a clear perception of an imperfection, but your behaviour has touched a raw place in them, so that their communication doesn't come through in a totally loving fashion. You are receiving a confusing combination of a legitimate message that you need to hear, laced with a quality of blame, which is not legitimate. This makes it harder for you to receive the truth in the message.

While the closing of her heart is certainly a mistake, it is equally a mistake not to listen just because blaming is present. Even if your partner seems to be in their ego when they are asking for a change, there may be, lurking underneath the blame, some truth you need to examine.

THE KEY TO ASKING

One of the best ways to improve the quality of your relationship is to learn the art of asking effectively for what you want. Those who become proficient tend to attain their desires frequently, while couples with difficulties in asking will end up not getting many of their needs met. As a result resentment can accumulate through the years and poison the relationship.

Two mistakes are commonly made. First, you may avoid asking for what you want. If past attempts to ask, dating back to childhood, have brought failure and unpleasantness, you may have formed a rigid conclusion that there is no use in asking. To ask, says this belief, leads to pain and frustration, which it is better to avoid by being stoic and resigned to not getting your needs met.

There are other reasons why you may refuse to ask. Perhaps, suffering from a lack of kindness to yourself, you harbour a belief that you do not deserve to have your needs met.

Or you may entertain the unrealistic notion that your partner should know you well enough to anticipate all of your wishes without being asked. Whatever the reason, your refusal to ask guarantees frustration and leads in the long run to resentment.

Second, you may ask in the wrong way. The most important factor in asking is the effect it has on your partner's feeling about themselves. In general, complaint, blame, criticism, or any negativity in your voice, however subtle, tends to elicit in others a feeling of guilt which shuts them down and renders them far less receptive to your request.

It is tempting to imply in your asking that your partner has not been doing enough. If Martha says in a slightly complaining tone, 'I've been really working hard all day long; would you mind folding the laundry?' I notice myself beginning to feel guilty: 'Uh, oh, she's the one who's been working hard and I haven't been pulling my weight.' I generally resist such requests. But if instead she says with a genuine smile, 'I'd love it if you would fold the laundry', I find myself more often responding positively. If you eliminate complaint or blame from your asking, chances are you will far more often receive a favourable response.

The way you feel about yourself comes through significantly in your asking. If you feel unworthy, your request may have an apologetic flavour, which can transmit the message that you don't deserve co-operation. Low self-esteem also breeds discomfort with asking directly. The alternative, an indirect and indecisive manner of asking, often feels annoying and manipulative.

On the other hand, feeling good about yourself will convey a comfortable quality to your asking, one that suggests you deserve to get your needs met and invites co-operation. In short, your attitude towards yourself will tend to elicit what you believe you deserve.

Be aware of the difference between a request and a demand. A request spoken with a harsh tone can sound suspiciously like a demand, even though most of us respond far less favourably to the latter. Some people in particular, often men, have a forceful negative reaction when they believe they are being told what to do. One way of avoiding this is to make it plain that it is all right for your partner to say no. In a healthy relationship, it's OK at any time to ask for what you want, and it's equally OK for the other to say yes or no.

We make a distinction between what we call the overhand and the underhand approach to asking. The former points a finger, overhanded, like an angry parent scolding a misbehaving child. It leads to resistance, both with your child and your partner. The underhand approach is a gesture with the palm up, using the index finger the way you would lovingly coax a hesitant one year-old to take a few steps. This style of asking makes your request more enticing.

The ultimate test of skill in asking comes with emotionally charged issues. Once you became more comfortable with asking it will become possible to convey, 'I want something, and I know it's hard for you to give it to me. You are not bad because you haven't given it, and I'm not bad for wanting it. Can we find some meeting ground where we could lovingly explore this together?'

SAYING NO

If you should say no to a request it is important to stay conscious of your heart. For years a predictable pattern would take place on certain occasions when Martha would ask me to do something:

Martha: You're going to town today?

Don: Mm hmm.

Martha: Would you mind calling to the bank and depositing these cheques?

Don: (in a weary, complaining tone): Look, I've got so much to do and I'm rushed as it is. I don't even have time to do all my own chores. If I try to squeeze in the bank as well, I'll be totally stressed out.

Martha: OK, OK, forget it, I was just asking.

Needless to say we both came away from such exchanges feeling worse. As we learned to keep our heart open when we said no, such dialogues began to sound more like this:

Martha: You're going to town today?

Don: Mm hmm.

Martha: Would you mind calling to the bank and depositing these cheques?

Don: (with a pleasant tone in his voice): I'm really sorry, I'd like to help you, but there just isn't enough time today. I'd be happy to do it next chance I get.

We are both left with a different feeling. With no need to explain, justify, or defend, the heart remains open. As a result Martha, knowing that she will feel respected whether the answer is yes or no, feels more relaxed in asking for what she wants.

However seemingly trivial this example may be, life consists of thousands of such moments. If both of you know that you deserve to get your needs met, that you can ask for what you want in a graceful way, and that your partner will take your request seriously and respond with an open heart, the emotional climate in your home will improve noticeably.

THE LOVING REQUEST

A loving request has certain characteristics:

Good timing. If your partner is upset, they are unlikely to be very open to hear you. It is a service to you both to take into account their emotional state when communicating something difficult.

Direct. Learn to ask directly and without apology for what you want. Instead of requesting, 'I wish you would hold me more often', try, 'Will you hold me now?' If you play it safe out of fear that you'll be rejected, you actually make it more difficult for your partner to see what you want. Naturally, they tend to retreat when they are getting mixed messages.

Explicit. It helps your partner if you can make your requests as specific as possible. When your request is broad and general it often comes across as too vague to be of much use. Instead of 'I'd like you to help me out more in the kitchen', try, 'I'd like it if you did the dishes and cleaned up two nights a week'.

Positive. It's also easier to respond favourably when a request is put into a positive format. For example, rather than saying, 'I want you to stop spending so much time with your friends and ignoring me', say 'I'd like to request one four-hour stretch of uninterrupted time together each week'. Ask yourself whether you might find it easier to say yes to the latter request.

Sensitive. If your request includes a perception of your partner's imperfection, be especially sensitive in the way you ask. In pointing out areas of unconsciousness or misperception, make sure you don't come across as blaming or patronising. This tends to corrupt your partner's sense of their own value, which may already be fragile. If you feel your partner could be doing better, be aware of how you would like to be told should they notice one of your own short-comings. At some level there needs to be the awareness that you are both doing the best you can.

Here is a request as it gets filtered through the ego:

'God, you were really awful at the party last night! You behaved like a mentally deranged two year-old after you had a few drinks. I can't begin to tell you how embarrass-ing it was for me! I really want you to stop drinking at par-ties, since you obviously can't handle the stuff.'

Here is the same request made from a more open heart:

'I'd be a lot more comfortable if you became conscious of the way you are at parties when you drink alcohol. Last night at the party I was very uneasy with the way you behaved. It appeared to me as if you went unconscious after a couple of drinks. You certainly said and did things that are not reflective of who you really are. This isn't the first time it's happened. I respect that you deserve to relax and enjoy letting go, but I would like you to take a really close look at what you are doing when you drink at parties.'

There is nothing 'bad' about people when they are uncoscious or unskillful. And, they might have richer, deeper relationships if they were more tuned in. Pointing out their blindness need not be a judgement; it can be an invitation to greater awareness.

Here is another example of a loving request:

'Last night when you told the kids to clean up the mess they'd made in the living room, I felt sad. You had a harsh tone in your voice which I think you weren't aware of, and it felt as though you were telling the kids they were bad, rather than that their actions weren't acceptable. I feel pain whenever you use that tone with the children, and you've done it more often lately. I know we both want the same thing with our children, that they grow up feeling good about themselves. In many ways you're a wonderful parent, and I know you were feeling stressed out and frustrated last night. I'd just like you to listen more closely to your tone of voice when you set boundaries with the kids.'

RESPONDING TO THE REQUEST

When your partner makes a request, do not get immediately defensive. We recommend treating requests as a variation of open-hearted listening. When your partner says that they have a request, take it as the same commitment to keep your ego out of the way, to mirror and to validate.

It helps to stay aware of your body and your breath, and say no to the urge to shut down. It also helps to remember that it's perfectly acceptable to make mistakes. They are perhaps noting one of your imperfections, but you are still OK.

Once they make the request, mirror back to them to make sure it is properly understood.

Then show your partner that you understand the emotional reality behind the request. If you feel defensive, your partner's request may seem unreasonable. In such a case make a very special effort to talk about the feelings which gave rise to their request, in order to understand with some empathy the nature of their frustration. See what needs aren't being met. It can be helpful to ask yourself what possible reason they could have for making such a request. When Martha and I ask ourselves this question we can always see some level at which the other's request makes sense. When you show that you understand what led your partner to ask, you are validating their request. Of course, this does not imply that you necessarily will do what they ask.

If you do say no, be aware of your style. You are familiar with the traditional response that says, 'What? Are you kidding? There's no way I could do that!' Naturally, your partner feels unheard and resentment is likely, which you will inevitably receive back.

Consider how your partner might feel if you responded in your own words with this spirit: 'I can see that you have been frustrated about this and I understand your frustration. Of course you would want a change and I think your desire is reasonable. For me your request in the form you gave it doesn't work, because then my needs aren't being met. But I am interested in finding a way for us both to get our needs met, even though we don't yet know what that way is.' The chances are greater for an eventual resolution.

Clayton and Heather found this approach practical. They were an active professional couple, without children, in their mid-thirties. Clayton loved golf, but felt guilty about spending so much of his spare time on the course away from Heather. His solution was to ask her to play golf once a week with him.

Heather, although she played, just did not enjoy the game. At first she considered the request unreasonable, since she had made her distaste plain to him. She was tempted to blurt out that she hated golf.

Rather than succumb to the temptation, she asked Clayton why he had asked her to play golf. When Clayton shared his feelings, Heather saw that he was really wanting to connect regularly by doing something physically enjoyable together. She told him that she saw what he really wanted, and although golf wasn't a suitable answer for her, she would try to find other outdoor activities they could enjoy together. Cross-country skiing and hiking proved mutually satisfying.

DEALING WITH DIFFERENCES IN STYLE

Differences in style frequently give rise to the wish that one's partner were more like oneself. A common pairing finds an orderly partner with a more casual one. This need not present a problem, unless resentment has begun building in other arenas. Then the orderly one may accuse their partner of being a slob, while the more casual one might denounce the other as being rigid and uptight. When differences are not respected, conflict results.

Winston and Helen were an older couple with deep New England roots. He was about 65, with a full and distinguished head of white hair, and the natural politeness that comes from tradition and ease with himself. Helen, about five years younger, had obviously put a great deal of care into her body and dress. They were a handsome couple, who had learned to step gracefully around each other's foibles, except for one issue.

'You never like to tell me what's bothering you,' Helen began, 'and it sometimes drives me crazy. So why don't you go first.' Winston smiled. 'You're right, it is hard for me to let you know that I am displeased. I was brought up to keep my uncomfortable feelings to myself. But this has bothered me for many years, so I guess I'm willing to let you know about it. You frequently get excited about all these 'new age' things. First there was macrobiotic cooking. Then it was yoga. The latest is rebirthing. Whenever you get involved in something new, it is as if nothing else exists; it takes you over completely, and you want to talk about it everywhere. Now I have nothing against this. I often enjoy watching your zeal. But I feel you make me wrong for my lack of enthusiasm. Many of these things just don't interest me that much.' Helen interrupted with an edge to her voice. 'I'm very aware of that. If you would only show a little more interest and not so readily dismiss what I do! I feel your mind is closed to new things. You make these subtly patronising remarks to our kids about my interests and I feel put down.'

'That's interesting,' Winston replied. 'I experience exactly the same thing. When we're with our children I hear you making remarks to them that imply there's something wrong with me for not doing yoga or rebirthing or whatnot, and I resent it.'

This was a new development for a couple that had managed for forty years to avoid fighting. We suggested that each make a request of the other, one at a time, so they could be heard. They agreed Winston would go first. 'I would like for you to be more respectful of my ways. I am more conservative than you are and am simply not comfortable with some of the things you get involved with.' At this point Helen started squirming. She wasn't used to being asked to change her behaviour and her body language was fighting Winston, even though she was trying to control herself. We asked her to breathe and to sit quietly with a receptive posture. She acknowledged this was difficult for her, but she made a good effort to relax and be present for her husband.

Winston continued. 'I want it to be all right that I have a different set of beliefs and values from you. And when we visit the children please be careful to be more respectful of our differences. I want you to understand that there is nothing wrong with me for differing with you.' Helen's ambiguity was clearly visible. On the one hand, she was grateful to have her husband speak what was bothering him after so many decades. On the other hand, she definitely had her own view of the situation, and felt Winston was being unfair by leaving certain things out. 'Well, I suppose I understand what you mean. You want me to make it OK that you are an old stick-in-the-mud ...' 'Come on, Helen, that's not allowed in this process, not even in jest,' I interrupted. '"Joking" remarks are often employed as unconscious forms of attack, and we encourage couples not to poke at their partners during the process.' She smiled. 'OK, you're right, I was poking a bit and I'm sorry. I understand that you want me to show respect to you even though you don't go along with my interests, and to be more careful and respectful of the way I talk about you. I think that's a reasonable request. You should not have to share all my beliefs and enthusiasms. I am willing to allow you your own ways and to watch my tongue around the children. If I forget, I give you permission to let me know.' Winston beamed with relief and in a courtly manner thanked his partner.

The next time we met, Winston agreed to listen to Helen's request, and she began: 'I feel an equal desire to ask of you that you show more respect for my interests. I'm aware that you don't share most of them and probably think many of them are rather strange. That's fine with me. What I don't like are the little innuendoes you make around our kids, and sometimes around our friends that imply, "Oh, there goes Helen again, off on one of her bizarre new age kicks. I guess I'll have to put up with yet another piece of weirdness until she outgrows this one ..." 'Come on, I think you might be exaggerating just a hair,' Winston interrupted. 'Hey Winston!' I interrrupted. 'That's not allowed.' 'Why not?' he asked. 'She was exaggerating! Am I supposed to just let her get away with it?' 'Frankly, in a word, yes. If it were you, would you want Helen to decide when you were exaggerating?' Winston heaved a big sigh. 'OK, I do know what that feels like. I'm sorry, go ahead, I won't interrupt.' 'Basically, I want the same thing you do,' Helen continued. 'I want to feel that who I am and what I like is OK with you, even though you don't personally relate to it. I want you to respect the path I've chosen, and to watch how you speak of my interests in front of others, especially the children.'

Perhaps as a result of Helen listening to his request, Winston was able rather easily to respond to Helen. 'I understand what you want of me. You want me to respect the way you feel the same way I want you to respect me. And you want me to refrain from subtle put-downs just as I wanted the same from you. You want me to show you respect in front of the children.' 'Not just the children,' Helen replied. 'Everyone.' 'I understand. You want me to be careful all the time how I speak about your interests and to respect them. And it's easy for me, especially after our last session, to see what a reasonable request that is. I would be happy to do that, my dear.'

WHEN YOUR PARTNER FORGETS

Many requests for change take the form of asking your partner to break a deeply entrenched habit. It is unreasonable to expect a sudden and complete change. Undoing a lifetime of mechanical conditioning does take time. Your partner will sometimes forget.

One couple we met used a signal to help remember. Marcy, a rather shy computer programer in her mid-twenties, had been with Jed only a year. They got along well except that Jed, a popular professor of English at a small college, tended to take over at social gatherings with his witty and insightful conversation. Marcy felt squeezed out, unimportant, invisible. She requested that he listen more and leave space for her to speak.

Jed acknowledged that he tended to monopolise things and agreed that he wanted to break that habit. Marcy said to him, 'I don't expect you to be perfect about this, I know you will sometimes forget. When you do, would it be all right if I reminded you? And if so, what would work best?' He told Marcy that placing her hand on his shoulder could be the signal for him to pay attention. Their agreement worked very well. Over time, Jed needed Marcy's hand on his shoulder increasingly less often.

If you are the one being asked for a change, you may sense the value of your partner's request but doubt whether you have the capacity to change. If so, ask for their assistance to help you remember. Now you have become real allies, joining forces to help each other live a more awake and conscious life. At our couples weekends we sometimes have people exclaim with some passion that they want a partner who accepts them the way they are. Should they prefer to maintain all of their unconscious habits, they will probably end up with a partner who harbours an increasing reservoir of resentment. They may become the recipient of nagging, withdrawal, direct or indirect anger, sabotage, or sexual shutdown.

You may have neither the desire nor the capacity to alter your essential core, but you can certainly transform the way you express it. In so doing you may reveal more interesting aspects of yourself and become a lot easier to live with. There is no person better equipped to help you in this noble task than your ever loving partner.

chapter 4

GIVING AND RECEIVING

What Spirit do You Emit?

Of necessity, we have emphasised transforming what does not feel good in the relationship. This is often hard work. A more pleasant part of intimacy is learning together what makes both parties feel loved and cared for.

I recently heard about a wise old teacher who spent years trying to discern which parenting style led to happy, well-adjusted children. She was acquainted with the parents of hundreds of children she taught and had carefully observed parent-child interactions for decades. In all her years of teaching she found one factor that reliably made a difference. Whenever the parents came to school to pick up their children there were some parents who expressed how glad they were to see their children. This was the factor that led to happy, secure children. These children knew they were loved.

A less dramatic example occurs when you phone somebody who has not heard from you in a while. Watch the positive effect it has on your mood if their immediate response is an obvious delight at hearing from you.

It is instructive to become aware of the quality of energy you put out when you first see someone, whether it's been a gap of five years with an old friend or just a day. When you first greet your partner at the end of a day, does your manner convey you are truly glad to see them? Imagine the difference if your partner imparted that feeling regularly to you. Often the first thing partners do on coming together is either to complain about their life or to go instantly off into their own individual worlds. It is good to share the things that bother you or to take care of your need for privacy, but on coming together try putting aside your private needs and complaints, so that you may communicate a basic feeling of goodwill.

Parting for the day is another especially good moment for being watchful. When you say goodbye to your partner in the morning, what is the last lingering quality between you? Whatever the feeling, it tends to remain with both of you for the rest of the day, colouring your moods and activities. Whether you part with a complaint, a casual peck on the cheek, or a deep, loving connection, you carry it with you into your day.

A dear friend of ours who had recently lost her husband to cancer was visiting. She told us they had grown extremely close the his final year. His dying had brought a great richness and poignancy into her life. I was leaving the house for the day, and Martha was preoccupied in the kitchen, so she gave me a pleasant, but rather perfunctory goodbye. After I left, our friend asked Martha, 'If that were the very last time you were ever going to see Don, would you be satisfied with the way that you said goodbye?'

APPROACH WITH CARE

Do you remember as a child when your parents would yell across the house or down the stairs, commanding you to clean

71

up some mess immediately? We usually have quite a few memories of someone entering our space and shattering our peace in an abrupt and harsh manner. When someone enters our world intrusively we tend immediately to assume a defensive posture. Often we forget to approach our partner awarely. Sometimes we burst in with a complaint, which is likely to feel harsh or abrasive.

The great Indian spiritual teacher, Krishnamurti, has suggested that the presence of a snake in the room would make us exceptionally alert. What would it be like if we were that tuned in when we first came into our partner's presence? It helps to note how it feels when our partner enters into our own space. The first few seconds of an interaction can set the tone for much of what lies ahead. Be mindful when approaching you partner.

WHAT DO I CONVEY TO MY PARTNER?

A skilful parent, dealing with their child's unacceptable behaviour, conveys a message that the behaviour is not OK, but the child's being is. The child, feeling safe and loved, will be more likely to receive the message. A less skilful parent will set limits with a scowl. Their body language, tone of voice and everything else convey that something is wrong with the child and they don't deserve love.

If you are not satisfied with the feelings coming from your partner you might ask yourself how often you smile lovingly? How often you acknowledge them? How often you appreciate them for fixing things around the house, for making tasty, healthy food, for going out into an often stressful world to bring home money, for keeping your clothes clean over the years? How often do you show them directly that you are glad to see them and happy they are in your life?

We are often unaware of the quality of energy we put out to our partner. If I am aware of the slightest nuance in their tone of voice, I can assume my partner is equally sensitive to mine. It would feel so good to me if my partner were respectful to me, forgave my mistakes and faults, appreciated and acknowledged my virtues. Am I this way for them?

The essence of an intimacy, happy or otherwise, lies in the hundreds of little interactions that comprise daily life. There is much learning when you bring more consciousness to these transactions.

IT IS NOT THE CONTENT

When conflict arises in intimacy it is seldom for the reasons we think. Partners who are upset with each other tend to attribute their negative feelings to the content of what happened, what was said, what was done or not done. In reality the major exchange of energy takes place at a deeper, non-verbal level.

Underneath the verbal exchange exists a whole world of communication, usually lost to the conscious mind. It can be found in the look in your eyes, the muscles in your face, your tone of voice, body language, and perhaps at a yet more subtle vibrational level. Your negative reactions to each other come, not from your words, but almost entirely from a perception at this deeper level that your partner is not wishing you well. In such cases disagreement easily becomes laced with bitterness and resentment. However, if you felt a loving quality coming from your partner, even disagreement can lead to a valuable mutual exploration in which your differences are complimentary rather than antagonistic, and the two of you feel as allies.

If you are to get to the very core of the feelings in your relationship, sink underneath the content to the non-verbal exchange. In particular, be aware of whether you are supporting or negating your partner's being.

THE ESSENTIAL MESSAGE: SUPPORT OR DENIAL

An elegant simplicity lies at the heart of your non-verbal message: either you are wishing your partner happiness, glad they are alive, loving them; or on the contrary, not wishing them well, withholding love, or passing judgement because they are unforgivably flawed. Each moment you are with your partner you cannot help but transmit one of those two messages at the most primordial level, through your smile or lack, the softness of your eyes, the nuances in your voice. Underneath the content, this feeling of wishing well is either present or absent, and here lies the essence of your communication.

You can become sensitive to this phenomenon if you start observing your inner responses in a variety of relational situations. How do you feel when the gas station attendant scowls, when a clerk snaps at you, when your partner's tone of voice has an edge? Notice how often you come away from such an interaction feeling a little less alive, more contracted, vaguely uncomfortable – the by-product of assimilating the energy of somebody not wishing you well. On the contrary, when you are with somebody who smiles at you or conveys good will, you leave their presence feeling a little more alive, happy, or whole. If you observe many such moments you may be surprised to find just how impressionable you are to the nuances of people wishing you well or not.

I observe how very sensitive our son is to the slightest affirmation or denial. And then with a little scrutiny I observe myself in Martha's presence. If she says something to me with just a hint of disapproval in her voice, or on the other hand should she merely smile at me, I realise that I, too, am affected to a surprising degree.

OBSERVING THE NUANCES IN DAILY LIFE

We all want our partner to treat us with love and respect. But are we putting out that quality to them? Are we sending forth a great deal of love and not getting it back, or are we in fact receiving from our partner pretty much what we are putting out? Those who are not satisfied with their relationship might look very closely at what they are conveying, especially non-verbally. Chances are they will find that they are not giving forth what they would like back. To see this can be a moment of truth.

Many of us wait for our partner to show us love so that we can then respond in kind. This is not unlike the Arabs and the Israelis, or other traditional enemies, each waiting for the other to cease aggressive actions so that peace may finally come. Although many opportunities exist to make the first move, watch how reluctant the ego is to do so.

It is quite revealing to start being aware of the nuances. If you have children, listen to your tone of voice when you talk to them. One hears a great many parents addressing their children with no respect. In fact, some parents almost always have a kind of negative quality in their voice when they speak to their children. Many of us had parents who forgot to engage their hearts when they talked to us. As a natural consequence we have developed a similar habit of communication with our own children, and perhaps with our partner.

Tune into the quality of your heart when you communicate about practical matters to your partner. Your message may sound cold, annoyed, or slightly blaming, or it can be conveyed with the heart engaged. Those who hear a tape or see a video of themselves are sometimes shocked to realise how little the quality of heart shines through. Those around us may get used to our style, but something gets painfully shut down in the process.

Everyone has a favourite mode of expressing discomfort and fear in relationship. Some have obvious anger in their voice. Some nag, or lecture, or whine. Some may become sarcastic, or cold, or numb. Others plaster an artificial coating of niceness. In all cases the lack of love is painfully felt at some level by both.

It is also useful to pay attention to the quality of energy in your home when you are not seemingly in relationship. Two people can be in different rooms in the house, each involved in their own activity, and yet there can be a palpable feeling of harmony and connection between them. However, in many homes the same arrangement feels more like two isolated people, walled-in and lonely in their individual pursuits. In some homes you can feel the heaviness of resentment without a word being spoken. That disagreeable quality has resulted from thousands of little negative interactions, stemming from feelings that have remained undealt with over the years.

Fortunately, there is no need to put up with such a painful circumstance. It is possible to learn how to clean things up as they occur. As your intimacy deepens, your mutual sensitivity will increase and you will both know when harmony is lost. Rather than resigning yourself to it, or using it as an excuse to blame your partner, or allowing it to spiral downward into serious negativity, you can say to your partner, without blame, 'I don't know what's happening, but I'm feeling that things are a little off between us. Are you feeling that way too? Do you want to re-establish connection?'

There is no need to make failure to engage the heart into another sin. A negative or uncomfortable quality between two people is but feedback, inviting investigation. In becoming aware together of all the unconscious ways we convey a lack of love through our tone of voice and other non-verbal means, we are helping each other to wake up and live with more awareness. Becoming more conscious of the subtle messages we continually transmit in our daily life may help to heal the emotional climate in our homes.

THE INSTANT REPLAY

One of the most useful tools for us towards this end has been the instant replay. If one of us says something to the other that comes across with a lack of love or respect, the other responds, 'Would you do a replay?' This is not asked combatively or sarcastically. It is an invitation to become more globally aware of the communication we have just given.

When Martha asks that of me I pause, breathe, and do a slow, careful replay in my mind not only of the words I just said, but as well the tone of voice, the body, and especially what I was feeling at that moment in my heart. Invariably on such occasions I realise that Martha wants to hear the same content, but with my heart open. It feels a lot better to me, as well as to Martha.

On some occasions I discover an unconscious negative feeling towards Martha that lies behind my unloving communication. Because I had been unaware, it emerged indirectly. In this case I now have an opportunity to communicate my feeling directly. What would normally have festered as resentment now has a chance to be made conscious and dealt with.

THE MUTUAL REPLAY

When I was a teenager I became totally enamored of the bassoon. I loved the way it expressed both the profound and the comic, and was fascinated by its capacity to move from an almost human plaint in a tenor register to a solemn and sepulchural quality in the bottom notes. I found an old bassoon, learned it quickly and later became a professional bassoonist.

In the act of learning, it became clear that practising is an art. To master an instrument you have to spend considerable time going over passages that challenge the fingers. Whenever you make a mistake it is necessary to focus on what was happening at the moment of error. It does not work merely to substitute the correct note and continue. You have to go back several notes before the mistake and play the passage awarely with the right notes. If you don't, you are likely to make the same mistake the next time.

Learning to be intimate is quite similar. In music you can tell a mistake if you know how to listen, because it simply does not sound right. In an intimacy, if you are able to listen, you can tell a mistake because it does not feel right to either party. Mistakes are moments of losing the way, forgetting, of responding without love to your partner. A mistake by one often leads to a mistake by their partner, resulting either in a fight or an emotional shutdown.

Unlike good musicians, who know that the mistaken notes must be corrected, intimate partners are prone to spend a lifetime endlessly repeating the same mistakes. Many of us are painfully aware how the mere mention of a certain topic leads to instant defensiveness so acute that no discussion is possible.

Something is needed to interrupt the mutual mechanical responses that lead us together into the darkness. The stubbornly conditioned mind sorely needs retraining in a different way of relating to its mistakes.

The mutual replay is a tool that has taught us much about our own roles in creating and perpetuating negative feelings. A hostile interraction requires two participants. If just one keeps their heart open a fight is impossible. Check it out if you have a child: should they come to you angry or upset and you respond with love, there is no real conflict. Whenever a negative exchange has occurred, there is always some point where each person forgot to keep their heart open and thus contributed to the same old weary, unfulfilling pattern.

Martha and I were driving from our home in Vermont to the coast of Maine, where we were to catch a ferry to an island in order to give a workshop there. It was a long drive. I knew that she had wanted to stop off in Augusta, where she knew of a restaurant where we could get healthy food. I had assumed she knew where the restaurant was. In an overstressed state, I was grumpy, and responded, as you will see, quite poorly. Here's what occurred:

Don: OK, we're in Augusta, where's the restaurant?

Martha: I don't know. We're going to have to stop and look it up.

Don: What? You don't know where it is?

Martha: No. Let's just stop at a petrol station and find a phone book.

Don: I thought you knew where it was! You expect me to drive all over a town I don't even know looking for some restaurant? Don't you understand, we're on a schedule. I don't want to even think about missing the ferry. We can't take the time.

Martha: Well! So my needs don't count, once again. You just get to decide what we do. I suppose we can have some delicious French fries and coleslaw at some greasy spoon. OK, drive on, and get your own way!

And so on. Does it sound familiar?

Most of us beyond the early, romantic stages of intimacy have experienced such exchanges countless times. An intimacy devoted to becoming conscious can make good use of such encounters. Instead of justifying why we closed our heart to our partner we can instead go back over the dialogue with a view to finding where each of us lost our way. Each has a chance for a separate replay. Our partner repeats whatever originally triggered our negative response, and we get to give a new response, this time with the heart open.

To do the mutual replay effectively it is essential to wait until after you have ceased harbouring negative feelings. After Martha and I had calmed down a bit, I did my replay first:

Don: OK, we're in Augusta, where's the restaurant?

Martha: I don't know. We're going to have to stop and look it up.

Don (taking a deep breath): Oh boy, I can feel myself beginning to get uptight. I'm concerned that if we have to drive around a strange town for a long time that it might cut our margin for the ferry close. I don't want to have a stressful drive and be worrying about time. What do you think?

Notice I didn't have to supress my feeling of concern, to pretend that I was feeling other than I was. Instead I located a different place in my being, where I could look at my fear rather than drowning in it.

For her replay Martha was able to greet my scared little boy with more compassion, while staying in touch with the integrity of her totally legitimate desire. Again, we went back to what triggered her to lose her way.

> *Don*: I thought you knew where it was! You expect me to drive all over a town I don't even know looking for some restaurant? Don't you understand, we're on a schedule. I don't want to even think about missing the ferry. We can't take the time.

> *Martha*: I understand. You're really concerned about not feeling rushed for the ferry. And I don't want us to feel rushed either. But I would enjoy a healthy meal if it were possible without feeling the time pressure. How about stopping at that petrol station and just asking? If it seems like it will be a hassle, or take a lot of time, I'm willing to forego it.

Not only did our new responses feel better to receive, they also felt a lot better to give. Paradoxically, much of our annoyance at our partner stems not so much from the way they are to us, but from our own disrespect to them. Why would we be annoyed at them for what we do?

When we act unlovingly to our partner we feel guilty at some level. Now their very presence reminds us of what we dislike about ourselves, and we end up disliking them for being such a reminder. The worse we act towards them the more we resent them. We then act even more unlovingly, which further increases our guilt. A vicious circle results which can lead to a complete emotional shutdown.

When we start responding to our partner with more kindness, it has the unexpected consequence of our liking them more. As we respond to their fear and hurt with an open heart, we feel better about ourselves, which in turn causes us to act more lovingly. Our partner's presence now triggers our feeling good about ourselves and our attitude softens towards them. The vicious circle has been transformed.

THE IMPORTANCE OF ACKNOWLEDGEMENT

One of the most effective ways of demonstrating this kindness is frequent acknowledgement of what we appreciate about each other. Most of us have spent considerable time in the world of criticism and negativity. Much of our conversation is taken up with observations of what our partner or others do that we don't like. A generally negative atmosphere is common in many homes. It is impressive how quickly acknowledgement can change this.

Many of us didn't have parents who frequently and sincerely acknowledged us. A truly felt acknowledgement can feel so good because we have been long hungering to hear an appreciation of our unique worth.

Some of us use false acknowledgement, or flattery, in an attempt to feel better about ourselves. Feeling unworthy, we are concerned that our partner will finally discover the awful truth about us and end up leaving us or ceasing to love us. One unconscious strategy for avoiding this catastrophe is to flatter our partner in order to win their approval. Such flattery feels uncomfortable to both.

For years I had trouble expressing appreciation because I confused flattery with real acknowledgement. I almost never told a friend that I really loved them. I was too embarrassed. My difficulty originated when I was a child. I would occasionally observe people who employed flattery in an attempt to manipulate others, to sell them something, or to purchase affection.

With a child's sensitivity I felt aversion to the lack of honesty involved in such behaviour. But then I developed an unconscious belief that all people who say nice things to others were manipulators and phonies. To this day it's not easy for me to express appreciation to a friend. It has taken me a long time to learn that when acknowledgement comes forth out of love, it feels good to give, and the receiver will experience it as genuine.

I love to be acknowledged by my partner. I delight when Martha notices my parenting skills and acknowledges me for being a good father. By reminding me of my genuine goodness, it helps soften self-dislike. Through genuine appreciation, freely offered, we can help each other heal our feeling of unworthiness.

Acknowledgements are more effective when they are specific. It is one thing to offer a child vague praise, such as 'That's a nice picture you drew'. It would be more effective to say, 'I really like the way you drew those clouds so fluffy'. In the latter case your child will more likely feel truly seen. Obscure pronouncements to your partner about everlasting love aren't effective compared to focusing on something you find special in the moment.

Look often upon your partner without the burden of the past. See their beauty, their suffering, their earnestness, their humanness, their basic goodness, and whatever makes them special. Allow yourself frequent moments of genuine appreciation, and then tell them what you are appreciating. Just as children need every day to receive the nourishment of acknowledgement, your partner, as long as they are carrying the wound of unworthiness, can use it as well.

MAKING YOUR PARTNER FEEL LOVED

Imagine if you made a list of how your partner could make you feel loved and they studied it seriously with the intention of making sure you felt their love every day. How much difference would that make in your relationship? How much easier would it be to forgive your partner's imperfections? Imagine the value of doing the same for your partner.

Usually it is the simple gestures that have the greatest effect. I love it when Martha smiles at me, offers to massage my head, makes something for dinner that she knows I love, acknowledges my efforts to change unwanted behaviour, encourages me to take time for myself, buys me a special little gift, suggests an overnight together at an inn, overlooks a mistake, or responds to my ego with love. Little demonstrations of care set the tone for a relationship and have immense power to dissolve negativity. Become familiar with the specific gestures that work for your partner and make a priority of doing them regularly. In addition, communicate in detail to your partner what makes you feel loved. When you both take the initiative to make sure the other feels well loved, the relationship will handle the difficulties with far more grace.

THE IMPORTANCE OF RECEIVING

Receiving the gift is equally as important as giving, for it completes the circuit. Many need receiving practice. When they get acknowledged they dismiss it, or they say something disparaging about themselves. Another way to avoid the experience of receiving is to praise the other back whenever you are complimented or are offered love. It might feel considerably better to the giver were you simply to receive.

If you have the tendency to avoid receiving, the next time someone gives you an acknowledgement, try simply looking the giver in the eye, breathing, connecting with your worthiness to receive, admitting the gift fully into your being, and say a simple 'thank you'. Remain for a moment with the feeling and be aware of the circuit that has been completed.

The great hindrance to receiving is the feeling of unworthiness. If you or your partner has difficulty receiving, you can be sure that feelings such as guilt, shame, or inadequacy are lurking in the shadows. In helping each other to receive gracefully you may be uncovering and dealing with some fundamental issues of self worth.

Sometimes Martha or I will notice that our gift to the other isn't being received. At such times our custom is to remind our partner that it is time for receiving practice. The gift is given again and this time consciously received. We have caught ourselves so many times in the act of deflecting gifts that we have become more aware of keeping that all-important circuitry open.

We highly recommend learning to receive as a basic act of self-love. You can't fully give love without loving yourself. Developing the capacity to receive will make your giving more complete.

chapter 5

AVOIDING INTIMACY

WHY ARE WE AFRAID OF INTIMACY?

MANY couples, wondering why their relationship isn't flourishing, blame their partner or themselves. In so doing they fail to take into account that, while they may crave intimacy, they are more than likely both terrified of it.

One side of us truly hungers for intimacy. We sense there is a great beauty in opening up our boundaries and letting another person in. To merge and blend as one is a fundamental desire. But our craving for closeness is matched by an aversion of equal strength. What lies behind the part of us that fears intimacy?

Opening our boundaries entails letting go of control and dropping defences. Most people are uncomfortable being this vulnerable. The origin of this discomfort can usually be found in the earliest part of life.

As infants we were originally wide open emotionally. Most of us were brought up by parents who loved us but not necessarily wisely. Their love was probably withheld from us when our behaviour triggered their discomfort. As a result we received a painful message at a deep level that we were flawed beings, at times not worthy of love.

From this unfortunate teaching our minds concluded that to be emotionally open led inevitably to pain. To protect ourselves from this pain we sent ourselves the message not to be vulnerable, because it's not safe. We became skilful at erecting a variety of defences against openness. In short, the part of us that remembers its painful early experience has some very good reasons to be afraid of opening to intimacy.

Our fear of intimacy is usually not conscious. Many of us identify with the part of ourselves that wants intimacy, and are not in touch with the other part. As a result of the conflict between these two antagonistic fragments, we may well be encouraging and opposing intimacy at the same time. Our unconscious fear of intimacy emerges indirectly in our adulthood through a variety of behaviours which we call escapes.

WHAT ARE ESCAPES?

Escapes are behaviours that allow you to avoid relationship. They are motivated by the often unconscious fear of intimacy. Escapes are not 'bad'; arising out of fear, they deserve understanding, not condemnation. Further, fighting against escapes would only give them strength. Instead, become familiar with them. By observing how the fear of intimacy displays itself in your daily life, you will detoxify the fear, which will then cease to have such a limiting effect on your relationship.

Like a garden, no relationship can flourish unless you put time into it. If you eliminate escapes you will find you have a lot more energy and time to tend your garden.

WHEN IS IT AN ESCAPE?

What is the difference between an escape and merely taking some necessary and well-earned space for oneself? The man who goes out to work eight hours a day may not be indulging in an escape. But in our culture if, lacking financial catastrophe, he finds himself working excessively and seldom spending much time at home, then he is more likely using his work as an escape. Whether or not behaviour is escape depends on whether one's motivation is to avoid relationship.

Is leaving your partner's presence in a difficult situation an escape? Not necessarily. If you are very upset and afraid you might say or do something you would later regret, it might be skilful for you to depart for a while, take a walk or do something physical, calm down until you get some perspective. If you then come back to your partner and indicate that you are now ready to deal with the situation, then you have handled it wisely. This is not escaping. However, were you in the habit of walking away as a strategy for refusing to deal with difficult situations, you would indeed be escaping.

If two people are in a healthy intimacy they will regularly spend time together. In addition, they will feel a natural desire to nourish themselves outside the relationship through time alone, friendships, hobbies, sports, volunteer work, and so on. Intimacy is enriched when both parties take what they find outside and bring it back to fertilise the relationship. This is not escape. Ending escapes means you spend your time either being in relationship or consciously nourishing yourself outside the relationship, but not unconsciously avoiding intimacy.

We want to emphasise once more, to stop escaping does not mean that you abolish caring for yourself and doing things that you love outside the relationship. If you are in doubt as to whether your outside activities may be escapes, check the following.

Take an honest look at your motives.

Examine the balance of time spent outside the relationship versus time with your partner when you both have the energy for each other. The majority of couples whose relationship does not feel good fail to attain a healthy balance.

Imagine that you suddenly were going to spend significantly more time together with your partner. What is your very first feeling (before the 'shoulds' arise)? Is there resistance? Fear? Why don't you spend more time together? Many who escape convince themselves that there isn't enough time for intimacy.

COMMON ESCAPES

We classify escape from intimacy in two classes. In the first category are all the things we do in order to avoid spending time together. In the second are ways of avoiding intimacy while being physically together.

1. *Avoiding Time Together*

Television is one of the prime escapes in our culture. Millions of hours of potential intimacy are lost to the tube! Many a foundering relationship would be well served if just this one escape were eliminated.

Reading is a wonderful activity for gaining knowledge, deepening perspectives, and relaxing. It can also be an escape. Many hide behind the newspaper each morning with a cup of coffee rather than starting the day with some kind of personal connection. Others spend far more time with a novel than they do in conversation with their partner. In our effort to be informed about the world, we may well lose track of how little we are informed about our partner.

The endless list of things to do: the grass needs mowing, the car needs a tuneup, the basement is a mess, clothes need mending. We all have things to take care of, big and small, and there's never enough time to finish everything on the list. But if we are in the habit of using escapes to avoid relationship, it's easy to use the list as a reason not to relate. If we spend lots of time on the list and little with our partner, perhaps it is easier to find something to do at the desk or in the kitchen than it is to confront our fear of intimacy. Since the list is a reality of life, we suggest setting aside regular time for our partner and putting it right at the top of the list.

Alcohol and other drugs can be a major escape. This is a vast issue, beyond the scope of this book. If you or your partner are using chemicals to avoid intimacy or anything else, it is wise to seek professional help.

Eating is another major escape for some. Not only the frequent forays into the kitchen, or becoming dulled by too much food, but all the extra time and energy spent on planning, shopping and cooking, when satisfying the palate has become a substitute for love and food more important than intimacy.

Children can be a common escape, especially for women. Children do require much quality time from their parents and many parents need to spend a great deal more time with their children. Nevertheless, check the balance of time spent between your children and your partner. Some women turn to their children when things get uncomfortable with their spouse. When parents escape from intimacy it is actually a disservice to the whole family. Children feel more secure when they sense a strong bond between their parents.

Work is a favoured escape for many. We know a professional man whose wife resents him for not wanting to spend more time at home with his family. When he does come home he experiences his wife's resentment, which does not feel good. Not surprisingly, he finds excuses to stay at work or to go to as many professional meetings as he can find, which breeds yet more resentment.

Sports, especially for men, are an easy avoidance. Many send a message that the private lives of their favourite sports heroes interest them more than the world of their partner.

Illness or tiredness, when all else fails, may be the only way we can find to avoid a painful situation.

2. *Escapes While Physically Present*

You can be physically present with your partner and still avoid intimacy in some of these ways:

Anger is not always an escape; it can be a legitimate part of intimate expression. However, if you find yourself frequently getting angry at your partner it may be a major defence against intimacy. The same is true if you find yourself habitually blaming your partner instead of seeing through their eyes.

Arguing or chronically taking issue are common responses when one is more interested in being right than in understanding the other's reality.

Denial of feelings or emotional withdrawal, while more common among men, are universally prevalent. These habits, usually originating in early childhood, are an attempt to escape from oneself, to protect oneself from guilt or other painful disturbance.

Relating with only the mind is more subtle, and sometimes less easy to recognise as an escape from intimacy. Your attention is focused entirely on the content of what you are saying, during which time you are missing out on your own and your partner's emotional reality. The brain is engaged, the heart is not. Men do this more often than women. But there is another way of relating where, no matter what you are talking about, you are aware of the flow of energy between you and the other person. In addition to talking about something, you are also relating with someone. Many a woman longs for her man to learn this way of relating.

Gossiping and other forms of distracting small talk are not often seen as escapes from intimacy. It is revealing to observe the state of our mind while we talk about what other people are doing. Perhaps, feeling discomfort at being intimately present with each other, we feel the need to place our attention elsewhere. Martha and I on occasion make an agreement to spend a period of time, such as a week, not talking about other people. There is a lot more silence.

Niceness is one of the more common escapes, yet it's often difficult to detect, since there is an ease and comfort to it. Through an unconscious mutual pact, partners who both like to avoid conflict agree to get along well at the visible level, burying whatever might upset the harmony. To the world it looks as if they 'have it all together', an impression they find comforting. The price of this surface harmony is the sacrifice of real depth of intimacy.

THE ULTIMATE ESCAPE

One escape from intimacy is like the ocean in which the fish swims: it is so all-pervasive that it goes unnoticed. If I examine my daily consciousness I find that my thoughts are constantly bouncing back and forth between the future and the past. This inner monologue keeps me from being present in my actual life as it is unrolling. The ultimate escape is my thought process. I observe myself to see if I am truly aware in watching a sunset, listening to music, taking a walk in the woods, looking into my partner's eyes. It becomes quickly apparent that if during these activities I am thinking, my attention is somewhere else. I am not really there. Because thought goes on so continually, most of us spend the majority of our lives not present. This is quite a revelation. [*See chapter 8, Mindfulness*]

One of the most common forms of thinking is planning for the future. Although some planning is obviously necessary, check to see how often planning is the mechanical escape of a mind uncomfortable with the present moment. An insecure mind attempts to achieve security by controlling the future. There is value in consciously choosing to live with uncertainty.

Staying with this feeling develops faith that one will be shown from within just what to do when the appropriate time comes.

When Martha and I take a walk and find ourselves escaping into the future, one of us may suggest that we confine ourselves to being present. By returning to the present, where our life is actually taking place, we find the sights, sounds, smells, and companionship of our stroll far more vivid.

COMMUNICATING ABOUT ESCAPES

It is common to feel resentment when you perceive your partner avoiding intimacy. As is so often the case, the two familiar ways of handling this feeling are polar opposite mistakes. The first error is to bury the resentment and say nothing, for fear of creating disturbance. This breeds further resentment. The second is to communicate from the resentment in a manner that destroys perspective. If possible, communicate about the feelings without being caught up in them.

We know an artist named David whose wife Rita, an editor, spent a great deal of time with her friends and little with him. David first expressed his resentful feelings in this fashion: 'You're always going out with your friends and having a simply marvellous time, but you never want to spend any time with me. You're so selfish that all you ever think about is having a good time, with absolutely no regard for my feelings. Sometimes I think I'd be better off living alone.' Obviously, communications of this kind made Rita want to spend even less time with David.

David was allowing his resentment to fill his being so that there was no space around it. This resulted in a communication so judgemental that it was difficult to hear the pain underneath. David needed to locate a part of himself that could create some space around his feelings, witness them, and then talk about them. He also needed to view the situation as a dynamic between the two of them, rather than something bad that Rita was doing to him.

When he was able to gain this perspective, David could now express a message with a very different flavour, while denying none of his feelings: 'Rita, I notice there's a common pattern we get into which makes me uncomfortable. You go off with your friends, then I feel deprived of intimate contact with you, and get resentful. Then it looks to me as if you resent me for trying to inhibit your freedom, and we're off and running. I want you to have enjoyable times with your friends, and I also want to feel nourished by our relationship. I don't think it has to be either/or. I'd like for us to work together to find a different way of dealing with this, even though I'm not sure how.'

The contrast between these two modes of expression made an important difference in the outcome. Without denying any of his feelings, David now offered an invitation to work together towards a mutually acceptable solution. By resisting the temptation to believe his partner was the cause of his unhappiness, he stopped coming across as blaming. When David talked about his feelings rather than using them to attack his partner, she was able to hear him without getting defensive, and a resolution began.

THE ROAD LESS TRAVELLED

Eliminating escapes can be challenging work. We are constantly given choices, one of which is more comfortable and familiar, the other risky and unknown. Attachment to the customary keeps us locked in limitation. When Scott Peck wrote *The Road Less Travelled* he expressed a much-needed truth. To take the road less travelled means to have the courage to make the less secure choice. In the interest of greater aliveness, newness, or truth, one has to enter consciously into discomfort.

Eliminating an escape, taking the road less travelled, is the less comfortable choice. However, another more insidious kind of discomfort results from indulging indiscriminately in escapes. Taking the road more travelled too often brings dullness and mediocrity, a life constricted by habit, imprisoned by fear of change.

Watch especially for escapes when one of you is in pain. Many have a tendency to pull away when they are hurting, physically or emotionally. It is also tempting to run away when your partner is upset or in pain. But times of pain can deepen your intimacy if you have the skill and the courage to create a spaciousness that makes the pain acceptable. (*see Chapter 7*)

Sensing the value of eliminating escapes, you might suggest to your partner to point out if they suspect you are escaping. Promise not to get defensive, but to check it out. A mutual investigation of escapes can lead to major personal insights, as well as greater depths of intimacy.

WHAT ARE YOUR PRIORITIES?

We often ask couples if they ever spend sizeable blocks of time together where they are just doing things they enjoy. For couples who are having problems, the answer is usually seldom. They say they are too busy.

Your behaviour is a direct result of your priorities. If keeping your body healthy is a high priority, then you will make time to exercise. If you say that you don't have time to exercise, what you mean is that exercise is not as important or interesting as reading the newspaper, watching TV, or whatever it is you do instead.

If you want to know what the priorities are in your life, watch how you spend your time. It can be very revealing. Is being in an intimate relationship high on your priority list? If you don't spend much quality time with your partner, then it's not.

What are your deepest wishes? If you were on your deathbed would you wish that you had done more business, become

94

more accomplished, had more experiences? Or maybe you would just wish that you had loved more. If your escapes are keeping you from fulfilling your deepest wishes, then you have found out something of real value. Perhaps if you determined your true priorities your escapes would naturally diminish.

TAKING REGULAR TIME TOGETHER

Taking regular time together is essential for the health of the relationship. Find time when you are alert and unhurried. You also need a stretch of time sufficiently long. Sometimes it takes a while after coming from highly separate worlds to blend into each other's energy field. An hour or two is better than nothing, but we find that it usually isn't enough to reach certain levels of depth together.

We find it is best to have at least four hours of absolutely uninterrupted time every week (if you have an infant, shorter, more frequent stretches will be necessary for a while). This means you're not dealing with the phone, with children, with things that need doing. Watching films or TV together, while perfectly fine, does not count here, because you are not really being in relationship. You might take a walk, go out to dinner, make love, engage in a massage, sit by a stream, or do anything together where you feel connected. A flourishing intimacy requires tending.

If you find yourself resisting the idea of regular weekly time together, explore the origin of that resistance. Perhaps you are afraid that painful issues would arise that would lead to conflict. Maybe you are afraid of finding out that you don't really love your partner, or they you. Or perhaps there are sexual fears. One way to evade confronting these painful possibilities is to ensure that you don't spend time together.

You are kept apart by fear of what would happen were you to come together. The longer you are apart the more fear says there may be nothing there. Over time the barrier between you becomes more thick and impenetrable. This is the same difficulty that confronts out-of-shape people who avoid exercise, because when they commence it can feel rather uncomfortable for a while. It may be scary to begin joining after a long separation. There is a need here for courage.

Perhaps conflict or deadness in a relationship is an invitation to awaken. Can you use the marvellous opportunity of intimacy to help each other become more conscious? Eliminating your escapes is a major step in this direction.

chapter 6

ANGER

ANGER IS A TEACHING

ANGER is one of the most difficult realities to face in relationship. When we look at relationships that end in separation, or get painfully stuck in perpetual conflict, or go dead, we inevitably find anger, whether in direct outbursts or simmering under the surface.

Throughout history humans have used anger in an attempt to get rid of fear and pain. Some of us have turned our anger in on ourselves, creating massive guilt. Or we have repressed our anger, leading to depression or illness.

Even though anger is often seen as a regrettable obstacle to a spiritual life, it is not merely an unfortunate aberration, simply to be eliminated. When you push away anger you are also stifling inner fire. If you are going to have true intimacy it is important that both parties agree to allowing anger a proper place in the relationship.

Like all uncomfortable traits, anger is not to be eliminated but purified and transformed, for in it lie the seeds for something of greatest value. In working together with our anger we act as alchemists, burning away the impurities and transmuting our anger into the purity of passion.

If you honour your precious fire, if you seek to know it and live it in a way that is aligned with your higher purpose, then you will not want to waste it by imposing it thoughtlessly on your partner. You will cherish your fire and use it for the good of the whole, knowing it arises from the depths of your being.

LEARNING TO GET ANGRY ... OR TO STOP

We are all climbing the same mountain, but we approach it from different directions. If your anger erupts with ease, redirecting it is your task. If you bury your anger, your initial work lies in feeling it and having the courage to express it.

Some erupt easily, frequently attacking their partner and trying to make them feel guilty. Those who are quick to anger often justify their feeling on the basis of how badly their partner has been behaving. They may in addition point out that repressing anger is dishonest and harmful and that it's OK to have all their feelings.

This attitude we have seen earlier as the psychological mistake. It is true that repressing negative feelings is harmful, and that anger, along with all other feelings, is perfectly valid. However, you cannot justify frequent anger and remain at peace.

Those who share this attitude need to create a place within themselves to view their anger with some dispassion. In the act of developing an inner witness to their anger they will learn how to stop indulging it mechanically. Their anger will become redirected as they become familiar with its roots in the past. It will wither as they challenge the beliefs and assumptions that underlie the blaming of others for their own discomfort and pain.

Others have difficulty expressing their anger, or even feeling it. For a lifetime they have been sitting on their rage, partly perhaps from genetic make-up or cultural conditioning, and partly because they were given a message as a child that it's just not safe to be angry. Such people seldom, if ever, allow themselves to get angry. In fact they are generally unaware of even having the feeling. In addition they may believe that anger is wrong, a vice to be condemned, or that it is unreasonable or unspiritual. We may recognise this as a form of the spiritual mistake, the undoing of which requires a very different kind of work.

If this is your issue, your first task is to realise that in your humanness you sometimes do get angry. This may not come easily if it does not feel safe to allow such feelings. When angry, all you may feel is a vague sense of discomfort, annoyance, irritability, withdrawal, or even numbness. You may need to ask yourself on such occasions, 'Could it be possible that I am angry?'

It can be valuable to enlist the aid of your partner, who may be quite willing to educate you about their perception of the ways you hide your anger. You might want to ask them if they ever sense that you might be angry without being conscious of the fact. If the answer is yes, encourage them to ask you at such times what you are feeling.

Once you begin to become aware of your anger, the next step will be to create a safe environment for its expression, and to take the risk to express it. Lacking this work, your anger will seep out indirectly, causing far more damage.

Neither way of dealing with anger is bad. The fact that neither feels very satisfying can be considered an invitation for change. And whatever form your work takes, it helps to agree on some basics:

It's OK for both you and your partner to be angry, acknowledging that it's sometimes very uncomfortable.

Work together to eliminate certain ways of expressing anger that bring unnecessary pain.

Explore your anger together, rather than assuming that if one of you is angry at your partner it is because the other is bad. It takes a great deal of awareness to prevent anger from turning into a mechanism of attacking and trying to make the other feel guilty.

ANGER FROM THE PAST

Anger will often erupt unexpectedly with a force that seems far out of proportion to the event that triggered it. In such a case the anger may have little to do with the immediate situation but represents something from your history.

We all bring a reservoir of ancient anger into our relationships. Once when Martha scolded me for being careless in the kitchen, I found myself in a rage, the strength of which truly surprised me. Martha's chiding had set off memories, deeply buried in the brain cells, of anger I had experienced as a child when I was unfairly (I felt at the time) scolded for making a mess in the kitchen. The pent-up feelings erupted with the force of energy long held in bondage and Martha was the recipient of what felt like a totally unfair outburst. Our partner's behaviour will frequently remind us of emotionally charged issues from our past, often involving our parents or siblings. This is called transference and in it lies the surprising strength of some of our current anger.

It is not only childhood that contains our reservoir of past anger. Old anger may also arise out of our adult relationships or from earlier times in our current relationship. If our partner has done something we have not forgiven, or acts repeatedly in a way that has bothered us through the years, our unforgiveness is stored as resentment. A look, a tone of voice, or a subtle gesture from our partner can liberate this dormant negative energy from our reservoir, which may overwhelm our partner with its unexpected strength.

Much anger in intimacy is old rather than current. One task of a conscious intimacy is for both parties to become familiar with their own and each other's past anger. This has value in two directions.

First, it is a great deal easier to accept your partner's anger seemingly directed towards you if you know it is actually old emotions being discharged. You will be less tempted to accuse them of overreacting, which is never a skilful response when someone is expressing a feeling.

Second, you can be of help to your partner when they are discharging their powerful negativity at you if you are able to redirect their attention to the true source of their anger.

How is this accomplished? One couple told us about an event which had just happened the day before. Nancy was trying to tell Dan something that had upset her about the children, and he seemed not to be paying much attention. Nancy suddenly got furious and accused him of never listening and not caring about her feelings. Dan, familiar with this work, was able to listen to her feelings without defence. After Nancy had fully discharged her anger and felt heard, Dan asked gently if she sensed that the anger was old and had a familiar flavour to it.

Despite an urge to continue attacking her partner, Nancy was willing to put aside the blaming portion of her emotion and sink into the raw feeling of rage. When she did so, she became aware that the feeling was actually that of the little girl, enraged because her parents continually dismissed and negated her feelings. Dan's seeming indifference had set off these deeper feelings.

Because she now felt heard, Nancy was able to feel and express some of this rage, while no longer directing it at her partner. Afterwards she experienced a feeling of release, like the clean air after a good thunderstorm. Dan had assisted her in the worthwhile task of clearing out the deeper layers of consciousness from stored negativity. Both parties benefited from seeing the anger for what it really was.

The more you explore your anger the more you are likely to discover that you are seldom upset for the reasons you think. Fearful emotions from the past, frozen beneath the surface of our awareness, cast a powerful shadow that darkens our present reality. Perhaps our anger is really the voice of the frightened child, believing they have no power.

At a more metaphysical level, our anger may be connected with the belief that we are cut off from the Whole, imprisoned in this separate body, soon to cease being. Fear is a continual presence with such a belief. Anyone would be angry at being dealt such a painful fate, given that our deepest truth tells us we deserve better. Our metaphysical anger is a loud NO! to the god who seems to decree that we are finite – an unacceptable limitation for infinite spirit.

INDIRECT ANGER

When angry feelings don't get acknowledged and expressed, they unfortunately refuse to disappear. Instead, they remain in the system, where they are capable of doing damage within and without. By turning inward on itself the energy of anger can become chronic disease, depression, guilt, fatigue, sleep problems, dangerous 'accidents', unaccountable failures, or other forms of self-sabotage.

Outwardly, the energy of unexpressed anger declares itself to others in all kinds of indirect and harmful ways. When anger is direct it can be an obvious teaching for both parties if they are willing to learn. But anger that seethes beneath the surface and emerges indirectly in its various disguises can be a more difficult teaching.

You express anger indirectly towards your partner in a variety of ways. You may close down emotionally or sexually. Indirect anger frequently emerges as passive-aggressive behaviour, the unconsciously motivated punishing of your partner by generating difficulty or pain. Typical passive-aggressive actions are regularly being late, forgetting to do things, or creating seeming 'accidents'. Indirect anger often comes out in a tone of voice that conveys a lack of love. It may emerge as a tendency to dwell on your partner's imperfections far more than on their beauty. Frequently it manifests as a tendency to get annoyed at trivial things. When negative feelings are not expressed directly, they come out indirectly in a thousand ways.

Indirect anger can be even more difficult to live with than direct anger (except physical violence). I prefer a burst of direct, no nonsense anger from Martha than having her simmer at me for a long period. Direct anger is like a visible wound whose symptoms call for instant action. Indirect anger is more like an internal haemorrhage, creating much damage before its harmful effects are noticed and dealt with.

Learn to recognise anger in all of its manifestations, so that it may be expressed directly. Then there is a chance for a real communication, providing the other person is truly willing to hear it. Indirect anger festers; direct anger can be released. Such release may also expand to include past anger, allowing the present to feel cleansed.

ESCALATION

A common pattern with anger occurs when each partner becomes angry at the other's anger in an escalating fashion. Dealt with unawarely, what starts as a mild annoyance bounces back and forth between the partners, gaining severity along the way, until it intensifies into rage.

For example, Martha and I had an appointment to go to our son's piano recital. She was late getting home from a previous engagement. She had recently been late for a couple of appointments and I didn't think she was going to be able to get herself ready to leave on time. I was mildly annoyed and expressed it indirectly by being a bit withdrawn.

Martha did not like my mood. We had been in a very loving state before she left and my sudden withdrawal for no apparent reason was hard for her. She began to get angry with me, expressing her feelings indirectly by criticising the way I had cooked the food we were bringing. I was upset by her tone of voice and by her emphasis on what I had done wrong rather than appreciating that I had taken time from several important tasks to do the cooking. In response my annoyance intensifed, I became louder, and blamed her for not seeming ready to make our appointment on time.

Martha, who had been keeping close watch over the time and had it all planned out to the minute, became furious at me for being unfairly angry with her and assuming she would be late. At this point she started screaming at me and finding me severely wanting as a partner. What had started as the mildest of disturbances had expanded swiftly into a volcanic fight.

Afterwards we could look back and smile at the familiar way the feelings had fed on each other and escalated. It so often begins with a look, a casual remark, or a subtly negative tone of voice. But when you are in a delicate or stressful emotional state, the ego loves to seize on what seems like virtually nothing, and to run with it. Your partner's fragile ego responds in kind by taking it further. Each gets angry at the other for their anger.

Here is a good occasion for more consciousness. Whoever had the awareness could have interrupted the escalation at any point either by letting go into a more loving stance or by requesting open-hearted listening. This is also a good occasion to go back and do a mutual replay. (*see Chapter 4*)

WHAT DO YOU DO WITH ANGER?

It is not always wise to express the anger the minute it appears. A sense of timing is important. There will be occasions to back off from the intensity for a period. Your anger may be so knotted, so full of tension and blaming, so completely inappropriate, that it may be better to take a respectful distance from your partner rather than to say or do something that you will later regret. And as you walk away, resist the temptation to judge yourself for being angry. Your anger, although it may be highly uncomfortable, is a valid part of the human experience, a piece of feedback with an important teaching for you. Don't try to rid yourself of the feeling immediately. It may help to find a quiet place just to be with yourself, making sure to breathe, allowing the feeling to grace you with its teaching.

On other occasions, when the confusion and turbulence are more manageable, you may want to share your anger. Here is where you will want to learn to make its expression clean.

CLEAN ANGER

The distaste we feel for anger is truly understandable, given our history of profoundly misusing it. But emotions themselves do not isolate, it is what people do with them that creates separation. There are very few role models for handling anger skilfully. We observe in a lifetime countless instances of anger with the heart closed, where righteous judgement prevails and the one receiving the anger is being attacked and asked to feel guilty. But there can be another kind of anger.

There may be times when someone you love persists in acting in a way you do not wish to tolerate. You don't have to pretend that certain actions don't bother you. You don't have to mask your discomfort with a feigned peacefulness. It is indeed a challenge to feel your anger without closing your heart. You have an interest, even when angry, in honouring your partner's being.

Have you ever watched a good mother, skilful and competent? She can get annoyed, even angry with her children, setting firm boundaries in a way that conveys, 'I really don't like what you are doing ... and I love you'. Even in the midst of their mother's anger the children will feel safe.

There is another, less skilful way of setting limits with children. We sometimes observe parents who convey not only, 'I don't like what you are doing', but in addition, 'You are a bad person, and do not deserve love'. Children who receive much of this kind of anger over time are bound to feel bad about themselves.

It is not difficult to perceive the difference between these two ways of expressing anger. One useful way of defining the contrast is to distinguish whether the quality of expression is clean or unclean. When you express anger to your partner, it is important to learn this vital distinction.

'Clean' and 'unclean' are not used here as value judgements. With clean anger you are as respectful as possible, without denying your feelings. Clean anger, while it may be expressed with force and vigour, restricts its expression to the feeling itself. 'I feel really angry when you don't keep your agreements!' It's a statement about me. I'm not pointing a judging finger at you, trying to make you feel guilty.

'I hate it when you do that!' is clean anger, while, 'You're so selfish, you never give a damn about anyone but yourself!' is unclean anger. The latter says you are a bad person, and is often accompanied by name calling, or absolute words such as always and never. Unclean anger is verbal attack, designed to hurt. Intimate partners who use anger uncleanly have a knack for attacking their partner's most vulnerable area, evoking extraordinary guilt and pain.

Anger may be natural when it emerges, only to lose its truth when it gets worked over by the mind. When anger first appears it has its own vital intensity, arising without a great deal of mental activity. But if you pay attention you will notice that after only a few minutes the raw anger begins rapidly to dissipate, at which point it undergoes a change in quality. Now the mind can keep it going only by justifying oneself and blaming the other. At this point, when the anger moves to the head, it begins to have an artificial, more toxic quality.

Learn how to distinguish between the genuine anger of the moment and the mind's later attempt to keep it going. Genuine anger has a clean and natural quality to it. Anger stimulated by thought feels less satisfying, more like an indulgence, and is likely to express itself as attack.

If the two of you see the value of transforming unclean anger into clean anger, then you can join forces to work on cleaning up your anger. Along the way you will have many opportunities to sharpen your skills. The time after a fight is particularly suitable to learn from what transpired: 'You were pretty good with your anger until you said I never give a damn about how you feel. That felt like hitting below the belt.' Confront the way you express anger, rather than the simple fact of getting angry. You have a more immediate interest in eliminating attack than in trying never to be angry.

Clean anger is a more practical and effective means of communication. When you are attacking, what will be most received is your own blame and judgement, and the threatening aspect of your message will drown out the content. The recipient of unclean anger will become defensive, creating an impermeable communication barrier. But in the act of learning clean anger you will find that it is possible even while angry to be aware at some level of your love for your partner. Then you will impart a quality that will make it easier for them to feel accepted, and they are more likely to receive what you wish to convey.

USING THE BODY

Anger, like all other emotions, has a physical as well as a mental component. The physical component is especially significant for those who are interested in releasing their accumulated anger. Stored anger is arguably more lethal than anything you take in from your environment or your diet. To clean up your inner environment it is essential to express anger and release its toxicity from your body.

Free yourself creatively. You may already have discovered that when you feel stuck, aerobic exercise or vigorous work can blast through stale or frozen feelings. At the end of a good run I sometimes become aware of previously hidden anger.

Yoga is another helpful tool in a different way. By opening up the body it keeps the channels unimpeded for all your energy to flow more freely, including your emotions. Furthermore, if you do yoga for any length of time you may find you have become more sensitive to subtle levels of feedback from the mind and body. By helping you tune into the nuances, yoga turns the body into a more sensitive barometer of your feelings. Some of the ways my own body informs me of changed feelings are:

Shallower breathing
Less erect posture
Tight facial muscles
Contracted stomach
Raised shoulders
Brittle voice

To elicit pent-up anger you can also scream into a pillow, allow yourself to have a tantrum, hit a couch repeatedly with a two foot length of rubber hose, or yell at the top of your voice when you are driving alone in your car. This is useful not only when you are feeling obviously enraged, but also when you feel a vague discomfort and suspect that you might have some feelings which you can't quite locate. Such expression is especially valuable when it's not suitable or possible to express anger to your partner, such as when you don't trust yourself to be appropriate with it, or when they are not present.

There are also a variety of exercises which effectively allow energy to move through the body and be released. Try working with a specialist, such as a Reichian therapist, or a person who does bioenergetic or Lomi work, or some of the many forms of therapy and body work that specialise in energy release. This is well worth considering, especially if your usual attempts to deal with your anger have not been successful.

If anger isn't released it will fester. If you use the body to move the energy, what was stagnant becomes a clear, flowing stream. To release yourself from holding anger keeps you from becoming bitter, mean, or contracted into a knot. You are honouring your vitality while restoring your sense of proportion. You learn that you can be trusted with strong feelings. When anger is present, expressing its energy harmlessly is a blessing for your health and for the well-being of those around you.

HEALTHY ANGER AND GOOD BOUNDARIES

If you have trouble getting angry, or repress your anger, it will probably be necessary to learn how to display healthy anger. Anger at times can be the voice of awakening, proclaiming something is no longer appropriate for you and that you must say no. If you are not heard when you say it gently, then you learn to express your message with more vigour until you get through. Anger can set a firm boundary as an act of self-love, proclaiming what you will simply not tolerate.

Your anger can be a real service to your partner if they have harmful patterns of unconscious behaviour or heavy defences. At times anger is the only message capable of penetrating such defences. They may need your fire to wake up.

Women in particular, being usually less physically strong, can benefit from being able to express healthy anger in order to establish clear, firm boundaries.

Once you are comfortable setting clear boundaries you can then learn to do so with an open heart. Setting boundaries lovingly is an art one masters only with practice. In learning when and how to say no, you may discover that it is possible to growl with such grace and love that your partner feels acknowledged and affirmed at the same time that their behaviour is being limited.

If you are the kind of person who avoids conflict, the voice of fear may argue that you have no right to get angry, at least under these circumstances. Such moments are excellent occasions to remind yourself that it is a gift to say no to your partner's expectations when they do not fit for you. Say no to what would hurt either of you or take you away from your path. You let both yourself and your partner down when you fail to say a resounding NO! on such occasions.

We are all climbing the same mountain, learning to make clear boundaries with an open heart. We climb it, however, from different directions. Some of us whose heart is more naturally open need to learn to emphasise making the appropriate boundary when it may be difficult to do so. Others, more comfortable with making boundaries, need to work on keeping the heart open in the process. In both cases the fruit of our labour is a rare quality of communication in which both parties are equally honoured.

CHALLENGING THE BELIEFS THAT LEAD TO ANGER

So far we have emphasised the importance of avoiding what we have called the spiritual mistake, where anger is condemned, repressed, or denied. It is essential to accept and appropriately express our anger, to understand its relation to the past, to find physical ways of releasing it that do no harm, and to understand how to use it for making appropriate boundaries.

In addition to learning the skilful expression of anger, another factor is needed if one is fully to receive all of its teachings. We have to approach anger from two different directions; the work is like freeing a stuck car by rocking it from both ends. Now we shift our attention to the avoidance of the psychological mistake, where anger is justified and indulged.

It may well be that the majority of our anger arises out of values, beliefs and assumptions that simply are not true. If this is so, there is a real necessity to investigate these false beliefs that support our getting angry in the first place. Perhaps if we become more conscious we may release these beliefs and have less need to be angry.

In photography there are certain processes that can only go on in the dark. If a light were turned on they would be interrupted. The mind, too, has its own processes which cannot proceed in the light of awareness.

For example, notice how often your anger towards your partner can be traced to blaming them for not being sufficiently loving – in other words, for being in their ego. Our ego has the hidden belief that their closing the heart is 'bad' and worthy of punishment. In the darkness of unawareness we justify the closing of our own heart, and get angry at our partner. Such a sleight of mind could only go on in the dark. If the light of awareness were turned on, and we could see clearly what we were doing, we would let the whole thing go in a burst of laughter.

Another extremely common hidden belief says that our partner is responsible for our state of mind, and has 'caused' us to feel bad. Those who investigate will discover that this is one of the most profound mistakes. Despite appearance to the contrary, we have a total say in the quality of our consciousness through the way we interpret our experience.

For example, much of our anger comes from feeling powerless. Parents' anger at their children often arises out of such a feeling. Some parents will plead, 'Please don't do that', over and over, until they finally explode in anger when their child repeats the same behaviour for the seventeenth time.

If this is happening to you, perhaps the universe is asking you to look closely at your belief that you lack power. Were you feeling confident and in control, if your child didn't respond to your request, you could get more and more forceful as needed, until you elicited what was required. Although you might need to express your fire, there would be no reason to close your heart.

Look as well to see whether you feel powerless during your anger. If you do, ask yourself if someone is causing your powerlessness, or whether the feeling is actually a belief arising out of your fear.

Sarah was angry at her husband Frank for not 'letting' her go out more often with her friends. Sarah's fear was actually saying, 'If I assert my independence it will make Frank really angry, and he may hurt me, or even leave me. At the very least he would show me less love. That would be intolerable, so I will resign myself to staying at home, and hold it in my mind as if he were a jailor who was imprisoning me. Then I can justify being angry at him for denying my freedom.'

Frank's behaviour, however fear-based and unskilful, was a cause of neither Sarah's feeling of limitation, nor of her anger. Sarah's own fear was the cause of her feeling imprisoned and angry. Without fear she would have told Frank all her needs, while remaining open to negotiate as an equal.

RIGHTEOUS ANGER

Anger is frequently accompanied by a feeling of righteousness. If you are aware it can serve as a warning signal that you are missing the mark. 'Look at what those awful politicians are doing. How could they be such terrible hypocrites? It really makes me mad!' This righteousness implies that I, of course, am free of the greed, self-centredness, inconsistency, insensitivity, or whatever inner state motivated their actions. Is this true?

One way of dissolving righteous anger is to become more aware of yourself in daily life, both outwardly and inwardly. Become attentive to the workings of your mind and heart from moment to moment, unflinching and without judgement. If you are also conscious of your words and behaviour, you may appreciate the essentially self-centred nature of your ego. The more you become aware of how your ego displays itself as insensitivity to others, unconsciousness, dishonesty, harsh words, judgemental thinking, closed heart, and lack of generosity, the more your realise that your ego is as self-centred, petty and vain as anyone else's. Egos, including yours, are all the same; they are simply not nice.

To see this clearly forces you into an uncomfortable position. Since you are morally on par with others, you have to blame either everybody, including yourself, or nobody.

Some traditional religious thinking, such as fundamentalism, leans towards blaming everybody. We are all sinners, it says. Justice requires that anyone so very self-centred, you or the other, deserves the most profound condemnation and punishment, unless they repent. To hold this view is to justify anger both towards oneself and towards one's fellow sinful humans. Guilt and judgement become a way of life.

Another viewpoint is possible. Perhaps all of us are merely confused, fearful, and in need of healing. Perhaps all this self-centredness is simply the product of a mind caught up in illusion, flailing about in its ignorance and confusion. If so, all fear-based behaviour, including one's own, deserves only a loving response.

Should the rational mind try to decide between the two alternatives of blame and compassion, convincing arguments might be given and authorities cited for whichever side one favours. But the limited and conditioned mind hasn't the capacity to discern matters of this nature; it is simply not equipped to do the job. Here the heart must lead the way.

We believe that the heart, when heeded, will realise that the behaviour which has triggered your anger arises from a fearful mind. Healing is needed here, not condemnation. The more you see yourself in daily life as you really are, the more the heart will prompt you to release the judgemental component of your anger. The more you learn how your own fears give rise to imperfections, inconsistencies and self-centredness, the greater will be your natural reluctance to blame your partner for their particular ways of expressing their human imperfections.

Of course you will still get angry, even after beginning to see the truth of all this. But now it will become increasingly harder to justify it. As the mind begins to puff up with right-eousness at your partner's failings, you will find yourself simultaneously becoming aware of your own similar shortcom-ings, and the righteousness will collapse. It will be easier to see that both you and your partner are little different at bottom from scared children, who deserve nothing but loving guidance and forgiveness for their fear-based behaviours. When your anger becomes purified of blame, you will feel it more as a sen-sation in your body/mind, and learn how simply to be with it. No longer supported by the mind's justification, your anger will move another step towards transmuting into passion.

DEALING WITH YOUR PARTNER'S ANGER

One of the most difficult challenges of intimacy is to be present and open to your partner's anger. For many years, when Martha was angry at me I had a powerful urge either to with-draw or get angry back. Instantly my mind would race to find something she had done that was worse than my own trans-gression.

When your partner is angry, withdrawal or attack fail to bring healing and only prolong the bad feelings. But if you can learn to listen without defence, in a place of pure receiving, you can bring resolution. This is not to accept that you are bad, or that your partner's view of the situation has more merit than yours. It is simply to acknowledge that your partner has a right to their feelings and that there may be a possibility for you to learn something of value from the situation.

Being present for your partner's anger is not easy to master. When learning to swim it helps to practice first in quiet waters before you can stay afloat in a raging storm. Practice being there for your partner when they are mildly upset and their feelings are not too threatening. Success at this level helps you develop a certain inner muscle, enabling you ultimately to embrace your partner's more powerful feelings as they arise.

Perhaps the single most important factor to be relatively comfortable with your partner's anger is your freedom from guilt, or the realisation of your worthiness. Only when you know your basic goodness can you hold in your mind and heart two ideas which up until now have seldom been able to exist together: my partner is really angry at me, and I am OK.

Most of us feel a profound sense of unworthiness. The more your partner gets angry or withholds love, the more it seems to prove that this supremely painful feeling of unworthiness is indeed justified.

Look closely at yourself when your partner is angry at you. You may begin to observe how swiftly their anger triggers defensiveness, a signal that shame or guilt lies beneath. Your guilt is not created by your partner's anger. Already present latently within you, it is stimulated into action by attack. Your partner seems to be saying with their anger that you are unworthy of love, a notion with which your guilt completely acquiesces. It is this feeling of unworthiness alone, rather than your partner's anger, that generates your discomfort.

The more you can become aware of your worthiness, imperfections and all, the more you will know in your heart that your partner's anger towards you is not a reflection of who you are. Then there is no more cause to become defensive, or blame them for becoming angry at you. You have no longer given them the power to define your worth. (*see Chapter 11*)

Remember also that when your partner is angry at you, if their heart is closed, they cannot be seeing you in the fullness of your spirit. They are actually angry not at you, but at an image of you they have manufactured in their mind, composed of bits and pieces of the past. Seeing this might make it easier to relax your defences.

Your partner's anger is likely to convey a two-pronged message: that you did something unskilful, and you don't deserve love. Believing both leads to guilt; believing neither, to a defensive state incapable of learning. It is good to disbelieve the second part, while listening without defence to learn if the first part has any truth. If it doesn't feel right, then you can allow them their anger, sensing the buried tension and pain they are trying to release. By letting them express it as you would a child whom you loved, you'll help them to get over it more quickly. On the other hand, if there is truth in their assertion, you have just learned something of value on your path to greater consciousness.

It takes the courage of a warrior to train yourself to be lovingly present for your partner's anger. It isn't easy work, but it is a profound gift to you both. If, over time, you are willing to hear your partner's anger without defence, your partner will come to trust you at a new level. In addition, you will be forging a vessel which is capable of holding all feelings and processing them completely. Certain kinds of important communications will now be possible for the first time.

When Martha gets fierce with me, a very human part of me may feel uncomfortable. At another, deeper level I rejoice, because I know what her life would be like if all these negative feelings had not been expressed. This awareness considerably softens my discomfort.

When your partner is angry at you, rejoice that they feel safe enough to express all their feelings with you. It is an honour to participate together in this extraordinary healing process.

chapter 7

THE ROLE OF PAIN

How we Become Wounded

FEW of us grew up in families where it felt emotionally safe to have and express our feelings. When we were very young our parents were God to us. Most of us had parents or parent figures who were not able to play this role of God in a way that helped us feel our fundamental goodness. Because of their own wounds, those who raised us felt threatened by much of our natural behaviour. In response they withheld love when we were crying, angry, sleepless, or any of the other ways that made them uncomfortable. We received the message, non-verbally as well as verbally, that these expressions of our humanity were unacceptable. We had it from the Ultimate Authority that there was something fundamentally wrong with us for simply being who we were.

In our culture there seems to be a special difficulty in finding a creative response to the exuberant energy of two year-olds, who are engaging in the natural and healthy practice of differentiating themselves from their parents. 'I am ME, not you!' they declare. By saying no they establish an identity different from yours. Unfortunately this declaration appears threatening to many parents, who have not learned how to encourage the child to have their own feelings, while making appropriate behavioural boundaries. Much of our wounding goes on around that age.

In addition many of us were emotionally injured by feeling unsafe in our families. A child is taught to be afraid in many ways, gross and subtle. A tension-filled mother holds her child to a tight body, sometimes with more irritation than love. A confused father, uncomfortable about his role, is often emotionally unavailable. An over-stressed mother fights more often with a father who hasn't the emotional resources to deal with a sudden diminution of attention from his wife. The child's privacy is invaded in a hundred ways, with no regard for the little one's dignity. A harsh quality in the parents' tone of voice becomes more frequent. Fault-finding greatly exceeds acknowledgement. In general the parents' fear gets transmitted to the child through an unpleasant quality in the home, teaching them that the universe is fundamentally an unsafe place to be.

PROBLEMS AT BIRTH

Many women of my mother's generation were loving, intelligent people who nevertheless allowed themselves to be taken in by the strange prevailing cultural and medical attitudes of that era towards birth. Go to the hospital and make sure your husband has nothing to do with the birth. (We heard a tale of one husband who found the only way he could circumvent the stern and rigid hospital rules against being present at the birth of his child was to handcuff himself to his wife and immediately swallow the key!) Drug yourself to avoid any pain, and in the process lose consciousness of the miracle taking place. Then allow them, without protest, to take your child from you, to exist mostly without being held or touched for a week during a most crucial time in its development. Every once in a while you may pick it up, but you are strongly discouraged from breast feeding. After you bring it home, hold it for a little while and give it the bottle when it cries, then put it down for four or five hours and let it cry as much as necessary, because otherwise it will get spoiled. Besides, lusty crying is good for its lungs.

It is hard to imagine how a culture could stray so far from anything resembling sanity. It sounds so bizarre to me now, for a mother to allow her own deepest instinct to be overridden by the notion that the doctor knows better. Yet we are all subject to the powerful pressure of cultural conditioning. How many of us in that circumstance would honestly have had the foresight and wisdom to challenge the prevailing notions?

Infants want so much to be held and caressed with love. Imagine the feeling of a little child being put down and left alone to cry.

In addition, the father's discomfort often adds to the wound. When you are born your father is the equivalent of nearly 18 feet tall. Gaze up to the height of near the top of a two storey building, and imagine a being that enormous looking down on you with fear, or strong negative feelings, or even violent ones. Consider the effect that would have on the tender psyche of the little one. That little one is you, and is also your partner.

From such experiences we carry into our adulthood the belief that this universe is not a safe place to be. And the feelings of fear, guilt, pain and anger live within, waiting to be healed.

SEPARATION: THE ESSENTIAL WOUND

Those who would heal will have no interest in blaming their parents for the pain. The wound that gets passed from generation to generation is nobody's fault. It arises from the primordial misperception in the human consciousness.

When we are born we feel at one with not only our mother, but with the whole universe. Our mind has not yet developed a concept of our being separate and distinct from what is being perceived. Undifferentiated sensation is all that occurs.

And then at some early point a most traumatic event takes place: we begin to regard ourself as separate from the rest of Life, a wave cut off from the ocean. I'd like to suggest that the profound fear resulting from this mistaken perception creates a great inner wound, the primordial source of our human pain. Passed on from parent to child, the wound spreads through the generations like a wave. In our personal psyche it expresses as fear, depression, illness and pain; in the world it manifests as starvation, war, pollution, or exploitation. (It is not necessary to agree with this viewpoint to do the work together of healing your wounds).

Only the light of awareness has the power to interrupt this mechanical transmission of the wound. We are here to shine a compassionate light on our childhood wounds, that we may use them in the service of healing ourselves and our world.

PAIN FROM CHILDHOOD

Why does intimacy so often arouse such ancient pain? To begin, perhaps it's our choice of partner. We often unconsciously pick an intimate partner who replicates some of the traits of our parents. Those with an alcoholic parent often select partners who have alcohol or other drug problems. Those with an emotionally unavailable parent(s) may choose a similar mate. The unconscious mind is using the relationship to reproduce the conditions of childhood in an attempt to heal the old wounds.

The unhealed pain from your childhood is likely to play a major role in the present dynamics between you and your partner. Virtually everything painful or difficult between you has some relationship to one or both of your childhood wounds.

When your partner acts in the ways you most dislike, you may be looking at an expression of unhealed childhood pain. For example, those who were emotionally abandoned as children will often test their partners continually, in an attempt to establish whether or not there is emotional safety. Knowing this fact may not solve everything, but it may elicit more compassion and understanding from the more secure partner.

How the Wounds Play Against Each Other

One partner's wound often triggers that of another, providing one of intimacy's great challenges. A couple we know had wounds that constantly aggravated each other.

Joan and Bill were an attractive professional couple in their late forties. Joan was likeable, intense, a bit driven. Bill balanced her nicely with a more relaxed quality, which sometimes felt as if it were covering over an unacknowledged passion. They had just gone through another one of their familiar blowouts, and they were becoming weary of the pattern.

The preceding night Bill and Joan both had important phone calls to make. Joan told Bill he could go first. Bill could not reach his party; but instead of immediately offering Joan the phone, he proceeded to call someone else, with whom he spent a good bit of time on the phone. When Joan realised what had happened she became enraged at Bill and started yelling at him the minute he hung up. Bill pulled back behind his wall, refusing to hear anything Joan was saying, because he felt so unfairly and overwhelmingly attacked for what seemed at most like a rather minor infraction.

As was so often the case, their conversation quickly escalated. Joan was getting increasingly angry: 'You knew I needed to make that call; it was really important. Why couldn't you have just given the phone over as soon as you couldn't reach Fred? I've got better things to do with my time than to wait around half the night for you to finish talking. I'm sick and tired of watching you day in and day out take such good care of yourself and act as if I don't exist! I just don't understand you.'

Bill looked as if he wanted to leave as quickly as possible. 'You can't understand? I'm the one who can't understand. I fail to see why you continually lash out at me as if I'm some kind of a monster. Look, I admit I blew it, I should have given you the phone, OK? But what I did wasn't that bad, and it most certainly didn't warrant your yelling and screaming at me like that. I have to tiptoe around my own home because I never know when one of your attacks will strike. I don't know if I want to live with someone who attacks me all the time for practically nothing!'

'Practically nothing, is it?' Joan responded, her voice rising half an octave. 'That's the trouble with you, you always dismiss my feelings. Every time I try to tell you how I'm feeling you always hide behind that dammed wall of yours. I might just as well be talking to myself.' And so on.

Of course, this is just the kind of exchange that open-hearted listening is designed to prevent. I asked Joan and Bill if this was typical of their fights and they agreed. They both seemed motivated to learn another approach, and picked up the process rather quickly.

Bill agreed to listen first. Just the very fact of entering into the process changed the expression on his face and his wall seemed to become several shades more transparent. Joan started out from her place of anger, telling him her story and finishing with the statement that she felt angry for not being taken seriously.

When Bill started to mirror back what Joan said her face became a bit softer. She was not used to having Bill present for her anger. After he mirrored her, Joan had a revelation. She remembered that when she was a child her parents did not take her seriously. She often felt ignored, or that her needs and wishes were of no importance. Bill's behaviour had stirred up her old anger.

Joan's anger now made more sense to Bill. He validated her: 'Making that phone call was really important to you. And when

I treated it as if it had no significance, it was just like your parents all over again. I was acting as if you didn't matter and your wishes had no value. I can really see how that would make you furious. I'm even beginning to get mad at myself!'

Despite her seriousness Joan burst into a broad smile. She felt validated and the tension between her and Bill was gone. They both understood more clearly how the intense charge behind her anger originated from her past. Now they had clarified an area of special sensitivity where they could both be watchful. The next time we met, Joan agreed to listen to Bill's feelings.

After telling his story, Bill expressed how scared he felt when Joan suddenly started yelling at him. Then he, too, had his moment of enlightenment. His mother had frequently got angry at him, often unfairly. He remembered how as a boy he could not understand what he had done to warrant such an assault. When Joan yelled at him after he hung up the phone, it was just like being a kid again, receiving a burst of unfair anger for virtually nothing.

It was apparent that they had both become more interested in uncovering the truth than in blaming each other. Now they were in a position to see how each of their wounds contributed to their ongoing conflict. Bill saw the source of her anger when he did not take her seriously. Joan understood why her outburst scared him and why he retreated behind his wall to a place of safety. Both their childhood wounds got activated by the other's behaviour, and they repeatedly had the same fight.

Having reached this level of insight, Joan and Bill each had personal work to do. Joan's task was to let Bill know of her upset without automatically going into an attack mode. She needed to stand outside her feelings, so she could talk about them without being overwhelmed by them. Bill's work was first to become aware of the ways he continued not to take Joan seriously, and second to struggle with his tendency to go into instant withdrawal when he is uncomfortable. He needed to be willing to listen to Joan's anger without pulling away, even if it sometimes felt unfair. They both needed to be willing to do open-hearted listening when such situations arose. Joan and Bill became vigilant around their common pattern and an awareness developed which brought a softening and a healing to the old wounds.

TRANSFERENCE

Those who wish to participate in mutual healing will want to become familiar with both their own wounds and those of their partner. This is done in a direct and experiential way, with compassion for the difficulty of both your struggles.

Exploring your childhoods together can be a fascinating journey. What did it feel like in your home when you were growing up? What made you angry about your parents? What hurt you? What made you scared? Are there periods devoid of memory? Is there any relation between what bothers you now and what went on then?

When your pain seems out of proportion to the event that triggers it (which seems for most people to happen a great deal) ask yourself if feels like an old and familiar feeling. If so, history is distorting the present. Present events, resembling childhood memories, stir up the embers of buried emotions. This phenomenon is called transference.

Understanding transference helps you to explore old wounds that were previously hidden in the dark folds of the unconscious mind. You must first experience a feeling to release it. The unconscious must become conscious.

If in a moment of discomfort you stay quietly with your feeling, it may reveal its message. At times it may take courage to remain with levels of discomfort from which you would normally try to escape. If you are a warrior, you will sooner or later come upon situations that lead you to your major issue.

Learn to stand outside your feelings and look at them with spaciousness. If you are totally immersed in your feelings, or identified with them, it's virtually impossible to get the distance needed for healing. If you can learn to lift above the battlefield and find a place to witness your feelings, if you can be sufficiently aware to realise that your buttons were just pushed, then you are no longer a slave to your feelings, and can begin to work with them. (*see Chapter 9*)

One man we worked with learned about this when his wife was late. Sean found himself getting extremely hurt every time Margaret failed to show up when she was supposed to. Even when she was only twenty minutes late his feelings would become quite intense. For a while he tried holding them in, which of course did not ease his pain. Then he allowed himself to feel the full force of his pain, which helped at one level, but the intensity was so great that Margaret did not know quite what to do with it. All she knew was that she could not possibly be responsible for such intense suffering on account of being a bit late.

Sean loved Margaret, and did not feel good about making such a big deal out of something trivial. Yet he realised that suppressing his feelings was not the answer. After being shown how to put some space around his feelings, and inquire into his past, Sean had a revelation. He was able on one occasion, instead of blaming Margaret, to stay with his pain. An old memory surfaced. His father used to promise to spend time with him and then not show up, which devastated him. Sean had felt there was something fundamentally wrong with him which made his father not want to be with him. He recognised that when Margaret did not show up on time it awakened the awful feeling that his father did not really care about him – that he was unlovable.

Sean's insight helped Margaret see how she was not responsible for his pain, but was merely a trigger. Now, with a little distance, she could be more help to him in his healing process. In addition, she realised that in being more conscious and reliable about time, she could help herself and her partner.

RESPONDING TO PAIN: THE TWO MISTAKES

Two mistakes are commonly made in response to one's partner's pain. The first lacks compassion and the second lacks perspective. Most of us have a tendency to err in one or the other direction and it is useful for both partners to become familiar with their imbalance, so that it may be brought into harmony.

The first mistake is the 'on high' response, aloof and devoid of charity. This attitude says that I am not responsible for your pain. You do your thing, I do mine, and if perchance we meet, that's fine. Such a perspective overlooks the beauty of the function we can have for each other. It represents a failure to take advantage of the rich possibilities for healing inherent in intimacy.

This perspective has often been found in conjunction with the well-quoted new age idea that says you are responsible for your experience. In recent times this notion has been misunderstood to mean, 'If you are in pain then you are to blame because you are causing it all to yourself, you idiot!' This is hardly helpful. Responsibility is not the same as blame. Even if your partner is causing themselves pain, they are most certainly in as much need of compassion as anyone. To be a healing force in their life is an opportunity to heal yourself as well.

The second kind of unskilful response to your partner's pain is to become submerged in their drama. In displaying great concern for their situation, believing in the soap opera, and treating it as a fully-fledged catastrophe, you are contributing to their fear by indulging your own and supporting in them the notion that they are in danger.

The inappropriateness of this response can be more easily perceived if you imagine someone responding to your own pain with upset and fear (I'm so concerned about you). Chances are you would feel more annoyance than anything else. When you fail to appreciate the value which the pain might have as a teaching, you have substituted pity for compassion. In your attachment to your partner's process taking a particular form, you have taken on their healing as if the responsibility were yours. You have forgotten their safety and your own, and are teaching them that fear is an appropriate response to life's challenges.

If your partner is caught up in their own pain, your best help is not to become similarly hypnotised and drawn into that vortex. Be aware there is a learning going on that neither of you may be able to see at the moment. It is time for trust that they are getting the appropriate teachings.

What does it look like if you are neither aloof and condescending, nor flustered and caught up in fear? To get a sense, consider how you would respond to a child who has just had a nightmare. On one hand, you would not give the child a pedantic lecture about the unreality of dreams. On the other hand, you would not whip up their fear level by getting dramatically upset about the content of their dream. Instead you might simply hug your child, acknowledging that from their perspective the pain was very real. At the same time, your relaxed manner and body language would convey to them, in a very tangible way, that they were in no danger.

Teaching safety is the most healing gesture you can confer upon a frightened child. It is also the most worthwhile message you can convey to your partner when they are in pain. While displaying compassion for the pain, and not negating it through some lofty spiritual ideal, you also communicate a deep sense that all is well. It is imparted through your smile, your touch, your tone of voice and the look in your eyes. The transmission of safety depends on feeling your own. If you can, your attitude will heal more than any words. The essence of how you can serve your partner in healing their pain is to transmit through your being that they are safe.

SHOULD THE PAST BE RELEASED?

What happens when a painful and traumatic event from earlier in the relationship interferes with the present? Conrad and

Anna came to one of our workshops with a classical dilemma. Many years ago Conrad had been unfaithful to Anna. She had been so devastated that she was unable to let go of her hurt and anger. Whenever Anna was really upset with Conrad she would bring up the incident, obviously feeling that at some level she had not got resolution. Conrad, who had apologised sincerely on several occasions, was now asking Anna to stop repeatedly bringing up the past, and start living in the present.

Both are in touch with a certain truth. It is natural for Anna to want understanding and release from her hurt and anger. Nevertheless, she needs to see that playing the wounded victim, making her partner the evil villain, will never bring the resolution she craves. She needs to convey to Conrad that, while she may have strong feelings, she does not want to use them to attack him every time she gets upset with him, and that she is willing to work on releasing these feelings and forgiving him.

It is equally natural for Conrad to want to be forgiven for his mistake so the shadow of the past ceases to darken his days. Nevertheless, he does need to realise that emotionally charged issues require patience, persistence and listening without defensiveness. He needs to convey to Anna that he has room for all her feelings, that he is aware some issues may require an extended time for healing, that he is willing to remain patiently with her feelings to the best of his ability.

It helped for Anna to bring up her pain at the workshop one time in a conscious way. Asking her partner to do open-hearted listening, she focused on her feeling, avoiding attack and blame. As her partner listened non-defensively she found that deeper layers could now safely emerge. Conrad was able to validate her feelings at a new level, and they both took a powerful step towards healing a major issue. Although she still did not feel complete, she saw the wisdom of letting it go for a period, and not bringing it up repetitively as a reaction whenever she felt hurt or angry. Instead they agreed to work together on building up the trust level in other areas of the relationship, and come back at a later time.

KEEPING THE WOUND CLEAN

Psychological wounds and physical injuries are similar. A minor miracle takes place in the daily healing of a simple cut. The process, which seems to be directed by a powerful intelligence within, takes place naturally as long as you keep the wound clean. No healing occurs if you pour dirt on the wound.

A natural psychological healing process takes place if you learn to keep the wound free of impurities, such as the blame and judgement which pervade our daily consciousness. To pour dirt on the wound is to be harsh on yourself or your partner, both for having pain and for the unskillful ways that you try to get rid of it. Given the prevelance of such judgement, it's no wonder that our wounds so often do not heal. Their healing would be greatly facilitated were the partners to learn together in an act of love how to keep the wound pure.

The heart is open until the mind closes it. Keeping the wound clean entails a willingness not to believe in all the mind's reasons for closing the heart, for harbouring judgement, resentment, unforgiveness. It means having the courage simply to be with pain, your own or your partner's, without moving away. It means finding the trust that an inner intelligence, without interference, can heal.

Stanley and Eve, an attractive young couple, appeared at our workshop. He was in his mid-twenties, gentle in manner with a rather sparse beard. She had long brown hair, wore a full, colourful skirt, and had a serious air. When they began doing open-hearted listening it became apparent they had been pouring dirt unconsciously on their wounds.

Eve's difficulty centred around Stanley's behaviour towards Tracy, their two year-old. He had the habit of suddenly grabbing her and picking her up abruptly. Eve felt that Stanley, even though his intention was pure, was being insensitive and treating Tracy too much like a 'thing'. This evoked some very disagreeable memories from her childhood, where

she was similarly treated. She took her mothering very seriously and felt judgemental towards her husband for not being
more responsible with Tracy.

Stanley was equally bothered by a habit of Eve's. While he
was speaking to her she would turn her attention abruptly
away from him and focus instead on their daughter, without
realising its impact on him. It felt to Stanley as if Eve regarded
Tracy as more important than he was. This, too, evoked in him
an old wound, in which he had felt invisible growing up in his
family. Hurt often turns into judgement. Stanley ended up
blaming Eve for being too uptight about her mothering, too
concerned about the child and not enough about him.

The more Stanley judged Eve for taking her mothering so
seriously, the more she reacted by turning her attention away
from him and towards their daughter. And when Eve blamed
Stanley for not being a more conscious parent, he was less able
to hear about his need for sensitivity.

When Eve and Stanley saw at the workshop what they had
been doing, each understood what was needed. Stanley told
Eve that he was willing to look at ways he might be more sensitive to their daughter. Eve told Stanley that she was willing to
look at ways she could be more sensitive to him. Both had
stopped pouring dirt on the wound so that it might heal.

BEING LOVINGLY PRESENT FOR YOURSELF

Helping each other to heal will have significance only if each of
you is also working to heal yourself. Although the expressions
of your wounds may vary, the work is the same for all. Simply
put, you learn to be lovingly present for yourself in the midst of
your pain. This may represent one of the greatest of all challenges. (*See Chapter 11*)

You may be struggling with a feeling of loss and emptiness
in your heart, resulting from emotional abandonment as a child

by parents who were unable to nurture you. Your old attitude might have been that you were not loved as you deserved and needed, so you were permanently handicapped by your emotional flaws and spiritual impoverishment.

It is possible to hold these same facts in a very different way: since you were not loved as you deserved and needed, you learned from your pain the immense importance of loving attention. As a result you are now especially willing to love and be loved.

If you feel sad and deprived, consider this your signal that the injured child within you needs support, and take it as your cue to do what is really nurturing for you. If you feel surges of anger at your parents, realise that this does not mean they are worthy of blame, but rather that your inner fire is engaged in burning up the old misguided patterns, that you may find in yourself the true parent you have always wanted.

Every committed love has its own discipline. As you undertake the discipline of being fully present for your pain, every instance in which you feel shadowed by old hurt will be experienced as a call to your deeper heart, and the wounded child will at last receive the loving attention they have so deeply craved.

What do I Need from my Partner?

Once you begin seeing to your own wounds, enlisting the aid of your partner will have a different quality, since you are not implying they are responsible for your healing. But they can serve in a useful capacity, especially if you have some sense of what you need when your wound is displaying itself.

Many people, especially men, believe being in pain automatically means that they are emotionally unavailable. This need not be the case, even if your history asserts that to be open is unsafe. It does, however, take a special kind of courage to be open to your partner when you are hurting.

When you are feeling your familiar wound, ask yourself what would be the most healing way your partner could be at this moment. Every time you feel hurt, angry, or withdrawn with your beloved, ask yourself what possible behaviour on their part would increase your feeling of safety.

If you take many such observations over time, you will begin to sense what might help. There are times you will require a wider berth for your healing and need to be left alone. Or perhaps you may want to be coaxed out of it like a young child. Sometimes you may need to be heard, perhaps through open-hearted listening. On other occasions lightness and humour may be helpful. And there are times when a special kind of reassurance is needed.

A couple we knew were going through a difficult time financially. Jim had quit his hardware business, finding it personally unfulfilling. Kathy had chosen not to enter the workplace in order to take care of their four children. While their financial reserves became increasingly depleted, Jim ventured half-heartedly into a few projects, none of which was successful. As their bank account neared zero Kathy showed signs of stress. Her normally pleasant manner gave way to increasing testiness. In fact, many of Jim's mannerisms which she had previously tolerated now became unbearable, and she was snapping at him and the children with greater frequency.

When Kathy told Jim that she was distressed about running out of money, Jim replied that this was a time for trust, and that everything would work out if she could just let go of her fear. True enough, but not the most skilful rejoinder for Kathy, whose irritability only increased whenever she heard such 'spiritual' advice. Something was decidedly missing for her in Jim's response.

As a child Kathy had often overheard her parents engaging in anxious conversations about their financial uncertainty. The little girl's natural insecurity was now reawakened by her current situation. What Kathy needed most was a strong, reassuring presence, a bottom-line feeling of safety.

Jim's first task was to listen to Kathy's fear of running out of money, play it back to her and validate it. But he also needed to reassure her of his commitment to his family. He was able to tell Kathy that he took full responsibility for seeing that the family's basic needs were provided for. When Kathy heard this, and felt Jim's sincerity, something in her was able to relax deeply, and her manner towards her family softened.

Both partners can become allies to help the wounded partner find the needed reassurance. The wounded one can ask themselves what they most need to help them feel safe. Their partner can ask if there is some form of reassurance they could give that would be of maximum help in their partner's healing. The discovery of the most skilful means of comforting your partner's wound is an art that can be fine-tuned over the years. Be sure to validate your partner's feelings before offering reassurance.

One of the most effective forms of reassurance does not involve words. Sometimes your partner's wound is so great, their perception is so clouded over, that their mind is completely confused. At such times words have limited use. When I am in this state, Martha will hold me like a child, with my head on her breast, which allows me to sink more deeply into my feelings. We begin in silence. After feeling more relaxed and safe, I may begin to talk about my feelings. Being held in this fashion can be a powerful aid in uncovering old hurts.

EDUCATING YOUR PARTNER ABOUT YOUR NEEDS

When your self-observation shows you what you most need for healing, you can begin to educate your partner about it. Inform them that when you become distant (or naggy, or angry, or lecturing, or whatever it is), that your scared child needs something from them. If you can, be specific about your need.

You may also be able to help your partner by encouraging them to explore for themselves what their own wounded child needs. Our friend George was able to do this with his wife Teri. One night Teri suddenly became sullen and withdrawn after dinner. George had just suggested inviting some new friends to come along on the hike they were planning. This seemed a perfectly innocent request to George, who was taken aback by her unexpected withdrawal. He pulled back as well and they went to bed on distant terms.

The next day George asked Teri how he could be of help when she withdrew. In this case Teri needed first for George to hear her feelings. It turned out that she had perceived George as being overly interested in outside activities and friendships, to the exclusion of their own intimacy. At last, when they had finally scheduled some time alone, George had wanted to dilute the intimacy by including others. Teri's little girl had felt hurt from want of attention and afraid she would never receive it. She responded by sulking and pulling away.

Because of George's interest, she could now get in touch with what had been unconscious the night before and share it. Once she was heard, Teri realised that she needed the reassurance that George was interested in spending more intimate time together. George was glad to give her this reassurance and they both felt a healing.

Two common ways of handling pain are either complaining or being stoic. The latter is more often the strategy of men, who learned when they were young that expressing their feelings did not bring the hoped-for love. Women often find stoicism difficult to be around. In fact the majority of women who come to our workshops wish that their partners would be able to talk more about their feelings. Similarly, men often have a hard time with complaining.

Neither complaining nor stoicism creates a comfortable environment. What does is the conscious expression of feelings, while putting some space around them. Martha and I sometimes employ conscious complaining, where we introduce our feelings by informing our partner that we are in a grumpy mood and just need to get rid of some emotional baggage. We then ask the other if they would be willing to listen while we release. With such a preface we find each other's complaining far easier to abide.

Find out what is needed for you partner's healing. Ask your partner what they would like from you when they are in pain. You do not always have to give them what they want, but know that when you do, you are helping heal yourself as well as your partner. If you both take the trouble to educate yourself and each other, you can become increasingly skilful at responding when your partner is confused and afraid.

Do not Respond to the Ego

When your partner is hurting you may be tempted to relate to their ego, the fearful, self-centred part of their mind, as if it should be reasoned with. However, there is no value in arguing with the ego at its own level and trying to convince it of its errors. This just serves to strengthen the ego and grant it greater reality. Your opposition demonstrates your tacit acceptance of the whole distorted thought system upon which it is based. There is no need to oppose what is unreal.

Rather than reacting to the voice of fear, respond instead to the spirit underneath the ego. Be like the x-ray, which cuts through the flesh as if it were not there and goes right to the bone.

It takes wisdom to see beyond the content of your partner's negativity. If the content is obviously insane it is relatively easy to offer compassion. If your partner claims you have green hair and two heads, and you're part of an alien plot to kill them, it is possible to distance yourself from the message because it is so palpably false, and respond to the pain behind the attack. But if, out of their pain, your partner attacks you in a way that hits closer to home, it becomes black-belt work.

When your partner seems to be rejecting you it takes some tuning in to determine their true need. Train yourself to slow down. Listen closely, the way you would to a young child who is telling you to go away. When my son was younger, during times of upset he would sometimes put out a surface message which told me to leave him alone. There were times when it was plain that he did not want me near him and I did respect that. But there were other times when I could tell that he really wanted me to coax him out of it. The trick is to discern the subtle difference between the real no and the no which is a yes. Listen carefully, underneath the words, to the nuances of non-verbal communication. Then you won't take your partner's seeming rejection as their ultimate truth.

Martha's responses to my wounds are so often effective because they speak to the part of me that lies deep underneath the disturbance at the surface. Of course her ego sometimes gets hooked, but she relates with increasing frequency to my essence instead of my ego. She takes me seriously without believing the story my fear has created. With room in her heart for me to be going through whatever I am feeling, she is able to smile lovingly at me in a way that lets me know that, despite appearances to the contrary, I am indeed safe. Every time I receive this gift I am freshly in awe of the miracle of healing.

BEING AT PEACE WITH YOUR OWN PAIN

Those at ease with their pain convey true safety. But most of us feel discomfort when we see our partner hurting. What is it that makes being lovingly present for their pain so difficult? What is the nature of the work that will allow us to do so with grace and ease?

The main key to feeling more comfortable with your partner's pain is to be at peace with your own. There is no magical formula for attaining this capacity quickly. It is the result of your willingness, over time, to resist the temptation to escape discomfort.

You are continually faced with the seduction of escaping unpleasant feelings through drugs, overeating, sex, entertainment, work, fantasy, rationalisation, or mindless pleasure. The more you resist or escape your pain the more strongly entrenched it becomes and the less likely you are to be able to receive its teaching.

When you resist pain it can feel quite unpleasant. Yet by itself pain does not have to feel so terribly uncomfortable, if you welcome it with an open heart. The worst experiences are more often the consequence of resisting pain than the feeling of the pain itself. Even though pain is by its very nature not a welcome guest, you can learn to move compassiontely into it rather than fearfully away from it. When you are at home with your own darkness, you are able to be far more helpful to your partner and others when they are suffering.

Consider as well how you develop the capacity to be compassionate towards the suffering of others. Empathy for another's sorrow is not possible without having first experienced your own. If your life had been a smooth and comfortable ride, it is unlikely you would have your present level of caring. The purpose of pain in your life has been to teach you to open your heart where it had been closed, that suffering might be transmuted into compassion.

Once you have accepted the value of the role pain has played as a teacher in your own life then perhaps you can allow that your partner's suffering is serving them similarly. We are not recommending the unskilful use of a 'spiritual' perspective to create an indifference to another's sorrow. It is possible to feel compassion for their suffering while at the same time not viewing the pain as something regrettable. If you partner is in pain, remind yourself that to be in pain is not the same as to be in danger. To be in touch with their safety, as well as yours, will allow you to convey the message that you both need to learn: pain is not to be feared, but to be held in love.

FREEDOM FROM THE NEED TO FIX IT

Being at ease in the presence of your partner's pain will also free you from the need to make them feel good.

When children witness the distress of their parents, whether it be through alcohol, depression, violence, or an unhappy marriage, the children will often feel personally responsible for the parent's misery, and develop strong feelings of guilt.

We tend to do the same with our partner. Observe yourself carefully whenever your partner is unhappy or unloving and see if there isn't some part of you that blames yourself. Perhaps, like many, you harbour the belief that your partner's unhappiness is a reflection of your own inadequacy. If only you were a better partner, lover, provider, if only you were more attractive, interesting, moral, your partner would find your relationship sufficient to keep them perpetually satisfied. Your lack, says this voice, is the source of their suffering.

If you have taken on this unhealthy responsibility to keep your partner happy, then each time they are unhappy serves as an unpleasant reminder of your inadequacy. Who would want to be around such a reminder? In fact, you may become downright annoyed at your partner for being in pain and thereby making you so uncomfortable. You may lash out at them, or you may close down to protect yourself from feeling yet more uncomfortable. If they could just be happy you could relax and feel good about yourself.

From this urgency to escape your own discomfort you may try everything you know to get your partner to feel better. It looks as if you are motivated by compassion for their suffering, but your efforts are laced with fear, and have a different flavour from true compassion. Such attempts do not feel genuine to your partner, for actions arising out of guilt are not healing. With every failure to alleviate their suffering you feel more guilty and more resentful towards your partner. You have entered into a painful vicious circle.

Men, especially, are conditioned to react to their partner's pain with problem-solving. Instead of simply being lovingly present for their partner's feelings, they habitually suggest either some action their partner ought to take, or a more enlightened way of regarding the situation. Such advice tends to sound glib and their partner doesn't feel heard.

To let go of the need to fix it:

Observe closely when you are hurting how inappropriate it feels when someone offers advice before truly hearing your feelings.

See with clarity who is responsible for whose state of mind. If you are able to suspect that your partner does not cause your feelings, then it will follow that you have not caused theirs. To the extent that you truly see this will you be freed from the false belief that it is up to you to make them happy.

Work to free yourself from your own feelings of unworthiness [a topic covered more thoroughly in Chapter 11]. The more you are in touch with your basic goodness, the more you can be in the presence of your partner's pain without it stimulating feelings of guilt. Remind yourself that your partner is in pain and you are all right. Although this may sound simple, it takes real work to create a feeling of worthiness independent of your partner's seeming well being.

As the two of you learn to accept both your own pain and the other's, trusting in the safety that lies underneath, you can create a spaciousness around the suffering and allow the intelligence of love to heal what has been so hurt.

Where Does Hurt Originate?

Although at one level the unskilful behaviour of our parents and others has wounded us, this is not the entire picture. The notion that another is responsible for our present pain deserves a serious challenge.

True intimacy requires that at least some of the time I have soft, flexible boundaries, that I be vulnerable. Most of us carry around the assumption that our vulnerability puts us in a position where we can be easily hurt. If I believe you are potentially capable of causing me pain, I am going to relate to you with a certain wariness. If I feel that I need to protect myself from your hurting me further, I will make myself invulnerable by hardening my defences. Common sense tells me that this gesture will keep me safe.

This would be true if my current psychological pain can be caused by someone else. But what if the source of this pain comes from my own mind? If this were so, then psychological defence against another is unnecessary.

One of the hallmarks of a spiritual relationship is to challenge the assumptions of common sense. I'd like to suggest that as an adult, you, and neither your parents nor your partner, are the source of your present hurt, which arises out of your feeling of unworthiness.

It was natural as a child to believe the messages your parents conveyed about your unworthiness. Since you hadn't the mental equipment to challenge these messages, they were in effect given for your tender psyche and could be said to have caused your wounds.

We are suggesting, however, that these wounds persist in the present not because of what happened in the past. You perpetuate their presence by accepting now the messages of unworthiness which your parents so long ago inculcated in your young mind. It is not the past wounding you now but rather your present acceptance of an old conditioning that has no more relevance. If you once believed your parents' evaluation of you was right, your continued belief now represents a choice you have the power to refuse.

If you accept your parents' or anyone else's evaluation of your worth, you are giving them the power to define who you are. As a young child it was natural and appropriate for you to give your parents such power. Now that you are an adult it may at last be time to take this power back. You no longer have any need to accept your parents' opinions of who you are and what is your worth. When you reclaim this natural right to define your own worth, you cease being a victim of the past.

A similar shift is needed with your partner. To the extent that you let them define your worth, you are severely limiting your capacity for intimacy. The fear of being hurt will dominate your mind and condition your behaviour. It is virtually impossible to be yourself, to act from your essence, if a major part of you is hanging back, protecting itself from the felt danger of an unfavourable evaluation from your partner. Is it your partner's behaviour that hurts you, as common sense dictates, or is it your own feeling of unworthiness?

Imagine if, while you were feeling good about yourself, some obviously disturbed little child, full of fear and pain, accused you of being an evil three-headed alien from Pluto. You probably would not feel hurt. But when an emotional child in the body of an adult implies you are bad, you may be convinced that they have hurt you. If you sound an E near a guitar, the guitar's E strings will vibrate in resonance. Similarly, if your partner accuses you of being bad, your feeling of unworthiness resonates to their accusation and you feel hurt.

It is easy to assume that your partner's accusation caused your bad feelings. But if you were feeling comfortable in yourself while they attacked you, there would be nothing within to resonate and therefore no source of hurt. A frightened child is crying for help and you are safe.

You may, however, take a close look to see if you might learn something about yourself from your partner's accusation. Perhaps their attack was triggered by unconscious or unskilful behaviour on your part. Feeling good about yourself does not mean you are free of imperfections or have nothing to learn. But it does mean that you have no need to lacerate yourself when you see that you have erred.

If you do not torment yourself, you will accept what may be true in your partner's communication, the fact that your behaviour was unskilful. At the same time you will reject what is false, the notion that you are a bad person for having erred, and deserve punishment. In so doing you will not feel hurt, even though you have been attacked. You may, however, feel a healthy momentary sadness, a remorse at having contributed to pain.

THE TWO PERSPECTIVES OF HURT

At this point you may ask if getting hurt is not a normal reaction. Getting hurt is a normal reaction, which we wish both to embrace and transcend. This requires holding together two separate views of hurt. The first view embraces both your partner's hurt and your own, taking them seriously. You learn to hold the hurt lovingly, do open-hearted listening, and investigate how you can be of most help in healing. This helps avoid the spiritual mistake, the view from on high.

At the same time, to avoid the limitations of the purely psychological approach, we are interested in going beyond the traditional, which is the domain of fear. The second view of hurt realises that as an adult you cannot be psychologically hurt by another. You learn whenever you feel hurt to challenge the notion that your partner did it to you.

It is challenging to hold both views of hurt together in the mind but it is essential if you wish to go beyond the traditional limitations of the ego and still remain genuine in your human feelings.

The radical notion that it is you who hurt yourself alters your concept of forgiveness. It is not surprising that the ego, loving to play at being 'spiritual', will take even the idea of forgiveness and distort it for its own purpose. How does the ego 'forgive?' First it feels injured, victimised, righteously indignant at what has been done to it. Then it pulls itself up and proclaims grandly that it has been hurt, but it will forgive. There is a patronising quality in this and a subtle attempt to make the other feel guilty.

A moment of honesty shows you that while remaining thus hurt you have not really forgiven. But with the new perspective you see they have not hurt you and therefore there is nothing to forgive. Here lies true forgiveness. As a couple you have the opportunity to practice this mind-altering shift in perspective every day. One of the great gifts to bestow upon your partner is to let them know that they are innocent of ever having hurt you. Nothing can be more invaluable in your mutual healing.

WORKING ON YOURSELF

Through much of this book we focus on how two people can bring more understanding and compassion to their mutual interaction. However, if the intimacy is to flourish both partners need also to investigate their own personal inner life, bringing these same qualities to themselves. Without this work on one's own, intimacy will quickly stir up the embers of buried issues, breeding painfully repetitive habits of relating. Working on yourself will illuminate old patterns and enable both partners to explore together with far more grace.

This private inner work is like a tree with two major branches. They are not totally distinct entities, for at bottom the branches are connected. But for the sake of understanding it may help to regard them separately.

The first branch involves learning to be more conscious, to dissolve old patterns of thinking and acting in the light of awareness. This requires being able to look freshly at what is happening both within and without. It means learning how to observe without the usual mind chatter, without history, without interpretation, without the usual likes and dislikes. The mind becomes spacious and can perceive with clarity. This way

144

of seeing has been called awareness, or mindfulness. We are also interested to explore how this quality can be encouraged and what gets in its way.

The second branch of the tree is to open the closed heart. It means recognising when your heart is closed and learning to forgive, to stop judging your partner, your child, your parents, the neighbours, the politicians, and events. And perhaps most important, it means learning how to be kind to oneself. Chapters 8 and 9 address the first branch; the succeeding chapters explore the second.

chapter 8

MINDFULNESS

The Importance of Awareness

In order to be in direct contact with the fullness of this moment, the mind, with its almost continual stream of thought, has to become still. If your mind is full of thought when you are looking at a beautiful sunset, you are not really receiving the splendour of the moment. The same thing is true if you are listening to a piece of music, or looking into your beloved's eyes. Thinking keeps you from awareness of what is actually taking place.

We move through the day with our mind almost continually occupied. We ruminate about money, sex, relationship, work, and a thousand trivial items. While we are thus preoccupied with our thoughts we are living like a person in a dream, walking through our life in an unconscious and mechanical state. Within this dream we create conflict in our mind, in our home and in the world. Those who sense the relationship between this unconsciousness and the problems in

146

their life will naturally become interested in waking up. A key to this awakening is awareness.

It is possible to work alone and with your partner towards a more spiritual life without being directly interested in the work of awareness. But we feel its exploration will help create a more conscious and loving relationship in a number of ways.

RELEASING FROM YOUR CONDITIONING

We all have conditioned attitudes and habits, passed through the generations from parent to child, that interfere with the feeling and expression of love with our partner. Many of them are distasteful. To become free of these reactive patterns requires that we develop the capacity to step outside them and see ourselves unflinchingly and without distortion. This necessitates freedom from self-justification (denial of our imperfections) or self-condemnation (guilt). Living in awareness helps us see ourselves with this clarity.

Particularly when we feel emotionally overwhelmed, it is important to have the capacity to detach from the melodrama of our relationship and simply to witness what is happening. There are times when our efforts to change can only make matters worse because we do not have enough clarity to see what is really going on. These are the occasions to take a step back – to breathe, allow and watch – and to refrain from becoming further entangled. The ability to let go of our habitual response is central to a conscious life. Awareness lovingly instructs us in these ways.

BECOMING COMFORTABLE WITH DIFFICULT FEELINGS

When darker feelings are denied or repressed they do not go away. Unexpressed negativity tends to fester and to create additional pain in its indirect expression. For negative feelings to serve their proper function, we must connect with them more fully. Learning the lessons that fear and pain are here to teach us requires developing the elusive quality of equanimity. When we no longer cling to what is pleasant and resist what is unpleasant, we develop the courage and strength to stay with what is disturbing without running away. What had previously been below the threshold of our consciouss mind can be brought into focus. Awareness hones these capacities.

SEEING OUR FLAWS CLEARLY

To be aware means, among other things, to become deeply intimate with our own self-centredness. Only then do we begin to see the great extent to which we participate in the very flaws for which we blame others. Being mindful in daily life brings into clear focus the essential sameness of all egos: ours, our partner's, and everyone else's. Thus we are released from feeling better or worse than our partner or others, and from righteous resentment. [*We will look at this more completely in Chapter 12*]

LIVING IN THE PRESENT

Awareness allows us to be more present for the fullness of this very moment. Much of our existence is spent with the uncomfortable sense that we are passing time, waiting for the curtain to rise on our real life, which will commence as soon as we find the right relationship, a secure situation, or some other ideal circumstance.

This widespread attitude has an unfortunate consequence. The present moment, instead of being sufficient unto itself, is treated as a mere step to the future, in which we place all our hopes. In the meantime, longing for the onset of our true existence, we amuse ourselves the best we can, while life passes us by.

Awareness reminds us as often as necessary that the significance of living lies right here in this moment. It will never be other than now. The effect on our intimacy is profound. Since real contact with our partner depends on our full presence in the moment, the practice of mindfulness allows us to explore at new levels what it means to be truly intimate.

CONNECTION WITH OUR DEEPEST TRUTH

When the mind stops its chatter there comes an inner silence, essential to receptivity from our deeper truth. Only with the ceasing of thought do we become sensitive to prompting from the quiet wisdom within that knows far more than the rational mind.

If you try to eat soup with a fork you experience difficulty. The thinking, discriminating mind is like the fork. It can probe, it can pull apart, it can analyse, but it cannot contain. This is the spoon's function, which is more like the intuitive part of your mind. It is not a question of choosing between them, but of using each quality of your intelligence where it can serve you the most fully.

Our intellect is best used for practical matters. Although it is an exquisite instrument, when it gets involved in trying to wrestle with the deeper issues of life it is completely out of its domain. Only when the rational mind is silent can we be receptive to the truth that lies beyond the deception of our limited conditioning. Awareness can be a gateway to an entirely new dimension in which things are not what they seem and the universe is recognised as safe and loving.

FREEDOM FROM JUDGEMENT

The most pervasive and stubborn obstacle to connecting with our deeper truth is our tendency to judge whatever we see as good or bad. Virtually all of our perceptions get filtered through this judgement, which occurs both consciously and unconsciously. The mind which is constantly evaluating according to its prejudices prevents a direct seeing of things as they are. 'The Perfect Way knows no difficulty, except that it avoids all preference' (The 5th Patriarch in the Zen tradition).

This truth is also acknowledged in the Garden of Eden. Mankind's stay in the simple beauty of paradise ended with partaking of the apple from the tree of the knowledge of good and evil. Although discrimination has its place in daily life, the mind must learn how to function without passing judgement to come upon the freedom it so powerfully craves. Teachings of every tradition attempt in their own fashion to depict this truth.

In watching the parade of outer and inner events without judgement, a quality arises which has been called the witness. In this state there are no opinions about the rightness or wrongness, goodness or badness of what is happening. There are no beliefs and values, nor is there a need to analyse. The mind is empty and spacious and regards with equanimity all that occurs as part of the passing show.

Once you have developed the capacity to witness you are no longer merely a pawn in life's game. You can choose where, when and how you will invest yourself in your relationship. You are free to live a caring, passionate, deeply involved existence without the fear of drowning in your own feelings, or of being consumed by the relationship.

Further, the witness plays a crucial role in the release of uncomfortable feelings. Trying directly to get rid of disturbing feelings is a mistake. Resistance, however subtle, guarantees that the feelings will be strengthened and we perpetuate what we most dislike. If you are experiencing something unpleasant, it's not possible to let go of it until you first acknowledge it, embrace its existence and allow yourself to feel it fully.

Change occurs not from your attempts to change, but from the pure light of understanding. A part of you is required that can stand outside your emotions, fears, beliefs, judgements or desires. The witness is simply aware that they are taking place and is able to embrace anger, pain, and fear. Your feelings are simple facts, greeted in an absolutely choiceless fashion, neither clinging nor resisting. Only then comes the understanding that leads to release.

RELEASING THE IMAGE OF OURSELVES

In addition to letting go of judgement, clarity of vision requires that the mind also releases its images from the past. Whatever we regard through an image, a symbol, a name, is not seen directly as it really is. Try looking at what we call a cat without the word appearing in your mind. You may catch a glimpse of something far more mysterious and interesting without the image from the past.

More challenging, look for a few moments into the eyes of your partner without the intrusion of the past. You may see them in a new way. Whatever you regard through an image will limit your perception to an interpretation, rather than to what is actually taking place. This is equally true when the object of your attention is yourself.

Through the years we have built up an image of ourselves, positive and negative, which we have a vested interest in maintaining. For example, many of us like to carry the image of ourselves as basically a decent and kind person. Whenever we have a stirring of dark feelings, our nice-person image becomes profoundly threatened. In order to protect the sanctity of our frozen image we develop inner mechanisms of denial that prevent these negative feelings from reaching our conscious awareness. Our vision of ourselves has now become seriously distorted.

Conversely, if we carry an image of ourself as fundamentally unloving, selfish, cynical, or emotionally crippled, we may feel too threatened to allow ourself to feel the genuine love which lurks underneath these defences.

Any image you have of yourself, whether it be positive or negative, will distort what you see. Therefore, your self-image is an extremely important subject for investigation. First become aware of the image, without making the fact of it bad or wrong. Then witness the image and stop identifying it as yourself. As you begin to see this image as one more occurence in your mind, rather than as some kind of absolute truth about who you are, the image loses its all-consuming hold over you.

AWARENESS

To perceive without judgement and let go the images of the past is a different way of seeing.

If you would like to explore this state of mindfulness, start right now to be aware of the feeling of your body. Now include your breathing in your awareness. Notice how this brings your consciousness more centred into the present moment.

When the mind has quieted down, your awareness, which began with your breath and body, can now broaden to encompass sights, sounds and smells. Explore these without the mind rushing to define what is going on. Notice how pure listening brings a quality of quiet alertness, especially when you listen to the silence between the sounds.

After remaining for a while in this state, broaden the awareness to include inner events: thoughts, feelings, fears, desires, likes and dislikes. Perceive how the distinction between outer and inner is actually just a creation of thought.

It is difficult to be aware when there is thought. Tune into the totality of what is going on in this very moment, without judging, analysing, or interpreting it. No longer are you greeting the present with the past. In this state of mindfulness, or awareness, you are open to learn a great deal about yourself.

MEDITATION

Meditation is an ancient spiritual resource, a means by which you can close the doors to the expectations of the world and the incessant craving of the restless mind, and turn within towards the source of life.

The quality of mind that watches in silence the passing parade of inner and outer events can be called meditation. Meditation can also mean the inquiry into the essential nature of the one who watches, the me, or self.

It is helpful to set a time aside for being quiet, for turning away from the seduction of the senses and allowing the chattering mind to settle. This permits your energies to harmonise, and a spacious quality of consciousness to emerge. We feel there is great value in spending time each day in such a state. In fact, when Martha and I begin our day in this fashion, which is our usual practice, we notice ourselves to be more conscious and in tune for the rest of the day. When we do it together, we harmonise our energies. If both members of a couple meditate together on a regular basis, they are likely to find that a new blessing will enter into their life.

Techniques abound to raise your energy, or to bring quietness, focus or balance. You may find value in playing with such tools if you are attracted. Concentration on the breath, or a word or phrase, can help focus the mind. Seclusion, fasting, sensory deprivation, or other forms of austerity can greatly intensify the depth of your experience.

Meditation is not merely sitting and doing a particular technique to the exclusion of everything else. Techniques are only ways of focusing energy and quieting the mind. The exploration of consciousness without the limitations of the ego is far too deep and subtle an activity to be reduced to mere technique.

What does it mean to function without a me, a self, an ego, a centre? In daily life the mind behaves as if this ego were an absolute reality. Most thoughts revolve around it, as well as fears and desires. All effort, all attempt to control and to find security, arises from this centre. All friction and conflict stem from this entity which calls itself me. Fear is the essence of this me. Wherever there is pain, anger, confusion, conflict, at the centre of it all is the me.

An old German poem says,

> Wherever I go
> I go too
> And spoil everything.

Is it possible for this ego to come to an end? Can consciousness free itself from the illusion of the separate self and function in an entirely different mode, without the conflict, fear and pain associated with this centre? Meditation is a way to explore this fundamental issue without any preconceived notions, through deep and silent questioning of the nature of one's true identity. Is there a me meditating? If so, who is he/she? If not, what is going on here? How does one inquire? Who is asking? Who or what is going to answer? A bit of investigation will soon reveal that if you employ thought to explore new territory, all you get is a mind playing around uselessly within the framework of what it already knows. A mind that turns its attention to itself will sooner or later come to see that thought will not go very far, and that another mode of inquiry is needed. There is no need, however, to make an effort to silence your thoughts in pursuit of a quiet mind. True silence comes when the mind ceases all pursuit, when it stops trying to grab hold, figure out, nail down, and control.

Even concentration, however useful for getting quiet at the start, can be seen as an effort of the self, because it involves control and it takes effort to exclude whatever you are not concentrating on. Any concentration of energy around a privileged point is still an expression of the self. The same is true if there is a goal. If you make a non-judging mind into an objective, then of course you begin to judge how much you are judging. That simply tightens the knot in your heart. With any goal, however subtle, meditation becomes but another activity of the self.

An ending is needed to all goals, thoughts, judgements and images. If the mind makes an effort to direct the investigation, that effort still arises out of the me. Freedom from the me, then, requires no effort, no control, no choice or preference. There can be no plan, no preconceived path, no technique or strategy.

What remains? If all activities of the me cease, all that remains is pure awareness. If you have gone this far, you can explore whether there is a self, a meditator who is meditating, a watcher who is watching the show, or whether there is just what is happening, ever changing, yet always in the now. You may discover that without the belief in the one who is meditating, all conflict comes to an end.

What happens to time in such a state? Without thought, where are the past and future? They are seen as nothing other than the content of present thought. In a state of mindfulness time comes to an end and you remain in the eternal present. Without thought bouncing back and forth from the past to the future, where is the me? It is seen to be an image from the past, having no more reality than a dream. A state without time is also without the me. All that remains is the eternal now.

Perhaps meditation had originally begun as another activity of the me. But now the seemingly separate self that got into this out of its own ambition or despair comes to connect with something vaster than itself. No longer can identity be defined so tightly, so imperviously, so rigidly. Consciousness, having let go of its images and self-conceptions, is now available to learn of its true nature.

THE MEDITATIVE STATE IN DAILY LIFE

In learning to swim you pratice first in calm, protected waters. Gradually you develop the strength and skill to swim under more turbulent conditions. The same is true of mindfulness.

It is relatively easy to practice being aware while sitting undisturbed on a cushion. Many who have developed this capacity, however, find that their prized equanimity evaporates with alarming rapidity when they are faced with an upset partner. Perhaps this is a message that mindfulness needs to expand to include every aspect of life, including emotional habits and responses under a variety of circumstances.

Once you have learned to become quiet when there is no distraction, you may then find yourself more frequently being in a mindful state when you are taking a walk, driving your car, or doing the dishes. Then, perhaps, you might find yourself maintaining mindfulness in the midst of relationship. Continued practice may allow you to remain centred during a mildly upsetting moment. Finally, when a disturbing moment of relational conflict explodes unannounced, instead of being totally reactive you will find that even here you may respond consciously. Such moments are great encouragements on your path to freedom.

chapter 9

ENERGY LEAKS AND DISCIPLINE

WHAT ARE ENERGY LEAKS?

The Russian spiritual teacher Gurdjieff likened humans to great balloons which have a constant supply of air being pumped into them. But these balloons remain only partially full due to a number of leaks. Our leaks are holes through which available energy flows out and gets wasted. This needless drainage keeps us from feeling fully alive and operating at maximum potential. It also keeps us from having the energy and focus to be aware.

All have their own unique leakage, with perhaps one or several major holes, surrounded by a larger number of minor ones. Typical leaks might be too much alcohol, overeating or poor quality food, lack of exercise, insufficient sleep, stressful work, stressful marriage, low self-esteem and frequent self-criticism, too much mindless entertainment, unprocessed emotional toxicity, or lack of real meaning in our activities.

Transformation involves plugging leaks, which increases available energy. Every time a leak is plugged our balloon inflates and we feel more alive. Any significant transformation must take into account one's own individual pattern of leaks. It makes little sense to put effort into plugging relatively minor leaks when energy is rushing out through a major one. To a person smoking two packs a day, eating organic brown rice is not likely to contribute much in the way of improved energy or health. But whatever the pattern of our leaks, our intimacy will suffer until both partners become familiar with their leaks and develop an effective way of dealing with them.

Agitation and Dullness

Energy leaks not only detract from the amount of energy, they also detract from its quality. We were designed to function optimally with a feeling of vitality, along with a quiet, calm energy. In most of us, energy leaks lead to an absence either of calmness or vitality. The first is agitation, the second, dullness. Both are imbalances that intensify the difficulties of living together consciously.

Agitation is a continual fidget, physically and mentally, that sends us racing ahead of our breath. We lean forward into the future with nervous energy (type A behaviour), and we are decidedly uncomfortable when there is nothing to distract us. A restless mind endlessly searches the future and past for comfort and pleasure. Agitation is being stressfully on the go, ambition, hedonism, tension and release. Agitation is rock music, neon lights, rush hour traffic, too much coffee, the need of a drink. In such a state one finds it virtually impossible to stop and savour the show. Agitation is favoured by the young and is found more in urban dwellers.

When we are agitated our natural bent is to seek further agitation in the form of amusement, drugs, projects, etc, until at last we weary ourselves and become dull. Or, tiring of nervous energy, we overeat, drink too much, or do something else to bring ourselves down.

Dullness, the opposite of vitality, is the feeling we all know that comes after eating too much. We are able to function but the spark of creativity is missing. Dullness is escape from pain into mindlessness, avoiding the intensity of the moment, with the predictable consequence of feeling less alive.

Dullness is watching too much TV. It is boring, repetitive work. It is too much alcohol and tranquilizers. It is a body lacking exercise, or staying indoors too much. It is comfortable, well-worn opinions and discussions about other people's affairs. Many of us, as we get older, begin to slide imperceptibly into dullness, which becomes the space we normally inhabit.

Sometimes, getting bored with dullness, we may begin again seeking out some pleasure that we hope will bring back the feeling of aliveness, only to return to a state of agitation. For many, this pendulum swing between agitation and dullness is the only quality of energy we know. When we have energy it is scattered or nervous, when we are calm there is little life force behind it. Seldom do we notice how both these common states help us escape reality by rendering us insensitive.

We make ourselves insensitive because we wish to feel less uncomfortable. A sensitive being will feel everything completely, pleasant or otherwise. Becoming insensitive is a classic strategy to soften the sharp edges of uneasiness. In the process, the capacity to be mindful is seriously curtailed.

THE SOURCES OF AGITATION AND DULLNESS

It is not difficult to discover the more obvious sources of insensitivity. Agitation is frequently the result of too much input or nervous animation. Watch the state of mind after any hectic activity. You will probably have difficulty being quiet, unless you have become exhausted. Too much loud or inharmonious music brings agitation. The media, with its overwrought pacing and excessive violence, also has an agitating effect on the nervous system. Constant talk, movement, disturbance and worry are agitating, as well as too much stress or change. Excessisve sweets create a jumpy mind. And, of course, certain drugs, notably caffeine, cocaine and amphetamines, help create a chronically agitated state in many.

Dullness is just as easy to trace. One of its chief sources is overeating. Not getting enough exercise is another, as is too much mindless entertainment. Overuse of drugs can also dull the system, immediately with barbiturates and tranquilizers, and ultimately with many other drugs, as reserves of energy are depleted.

Habitual patterns of thought and behaviour bring dullness. Just as too much change breeds agitation, too little variety in activity and freshness in perspective fosters dullness. Dullness is also an early warning for disease and premature ageing. And finally, a most tragic source of dullness is a fundamental lack of interest in one's work or meaning in one's life.

In resigning ourselves to living in agitation and dullness, we have forgotten their original purpose, simply as feedback that the system is out of balance. A balanced person, neither agitated nor dull, has an abundance of energy, like a fine, well-tuned engine in neutral. Calm and centred, the energy springs instantly to life when there is challenge, returning to quiet when the challenge is over. The system is alert, at peace with itself, harmonious and capable of real creativity.

Without realising it, we long for this balance. We desire both vitality (the absence of dullness) and peace (the absence of agitation). The difficulty comes from our tendency to misread the feedback that tells us the system is out of balance.

LISTENING TO FEEDBACK

At every moment our system, like all of life, self-corrects disharmony by sending itself messages about its state. These messages are designed to help the system maintain balance amidst
the movement of constant outer and inner change. Their function is to alert the organism to action whenever it is out of balance. An example of this principle is found in the thermostat.
Whenever it goes beyond certain limits the mechanism is
designed to turn itself on or off, in order to get back within the
desired range. The process by which the living being lets itself
know how its systems are functioning is called feedback. Its
proper functioning plays a vital role in living harmoniously.

When we are thirsty or cold, the body is sending a message
to the mind to pay attention. Something needs to come back
into harmony. If we listen properly to this feedback, we take
some sort of action, such as drinking some water or putting on
a sweater, to rectify the imbalance.

While we are normally aware of the grosser forms of feedback, we have not been educated to appreciate the nuances of the
more subtle varieties. Agitation and dullness are not generally
recognised as a message indicating something is out of balance.
When these states arise we try to escape from their discomfort. We
would do better listening carefully to the feedback they may be
bringing us about our lifestyle, habits, or recent behaviour, with
the spirit of rectifying the imbalance. For example, when we feel
dull we may go for caffeine or sugar, which does bring energy. We
pay, however, first with agitation and then with even greater dullness. Or when we are agitated, we reach for a drink, which may
pacify the nervous system, but may have an adverse impact on
the body and mind and lead sooner or later to dullness.

Nature has designed discomfort as an efficient way of getting our attention. Because we have not learned this lesson, our
traditional responses to agitation and dullness tend to create
more of the same.

161

We often ignore the early warnings from our system. For example, a man may disregard a feeling of chronic tiredness, or frequent colds or aches, or waking up dispirited. In the next stage the feedback may become more intense. This man may now get pneumonia, or perhaps become involved in a moderately serious accident, again nature's way of asking him to pay attention. If the second level of feedback goes unheeded, the volume gets turned even higher. The next stage might be a heart attack, cancer, or a very serious accident.

Disharmony always gives signals. If we are able to learn the art of listening to our feedback, then lessons do not have to be so painful. But when pain comes, it can be a blessing in disguise, because it has the capacity to shake us loose from something we are needing to release. Crisis is often the result of resistance to change.

ENERGY LEAKS AND TOTAL DIET

A relationship that breaks free from the prison of the past requires awareness. You cannot do the work of transformation while you are unconscious. Agitation and dullness both make being conscious quite arduous. When you are moving fast, it's hard to appreciate the scenery; when the mind is racing, it's difficult to be in touch with the present. It is similarly difficult to be alert and conscious when the mind is dull, because real consciousness requires energy. When you are agitated or dull you simply forget to be conscious. These states can be seen as hindrances to a conscious relationship.

It's also not that interesting to be in relationship with someone who is too agitated or dull to be alert and present. Therefore, in the interest of high quality intimacy, it is worth investigating how to transform these qualities. The key lies in learning to plug energy leaks through awareness of your time alone and in contact with nature, entertainment, music and reading material.

It may seem strange at first to consider the sights and sounds of the world as food. Yet consider the total effect on your being if you spend a week in the mountains, taking in the fresh mountain air, the vast and inspiring panorama, the rustle of the wind against a backdrop of deep silence. This is food of the highest quality, nourishing and healing.

Consider next another week spent in clamorous factories, rush hour traffic, smoky bars, or chaotic homes filled with blaring music, TV and relational dissonance. Just as the organism is able to function on junk food, but far less efficiently, so is its function correspondingly impaired by unharmonious sense impressions. Everything that we take in gets digested and turned into consciousness whose quality reflects the nature of the input.

If you want to begin changing the quality of your consciousness, take a careful look at your total diet. There are total diets that inspire more awareness, and those that encourage forgetting. If you and your partner are serious about leading a more conscious life together, you may want to review your total diet for a typical week and ask yourselves if it is in alignment with your deepest purpose.

Most people have developed their own personal assortment of self-destructive habits, or ways of not being true to themselves. These may include irresponsible eating, lack of exercise, chronic emotional withdrawal, substance addiction, not taking time for oneself, self-pity, and other forms of disrespect to oneself. It is not our interest to pass judgement on these habits, but rather to examine their effect on consiousness.

Seeing to physical leaks is likely to make a significant difference for almost everyone. These may include relationship to food, exercise and chemicals. This is often a good place to begin focusing for those whose lives are crystallised into a holding pattern. Bodily leaks, being more tangible and visible, are frequently easier to work with than mental ones. Also, the results of healthier living are soon noticed. A modest change is inspiration for further progress.

Some Common Energy Leaks

Note the significant overlap between traditional escapes from intimacy and common energy leaks.

Incessant activity. Many don't know what it feels like to have their organism running healthily, because it is overheated from running ceaselessly. We work hard and we play hard, but other than when we are exhausted, we rarely stop activity altogether. In fact the thought never even occurs to us. Too seldom do we sit under a tree and watch the clouds, or quietly nourish ourselves with the ever-changing music of a stream. Many of us would plug a significant energy leak if we balanced our doing with more being.

There is a rhythm between the outward and the inward flow, between making contact with others and resting, between expressing yourself and withdrawing. When your energy moves according to this natural rhythm, you are restored by your experience both of action and of rest.

Poor eating habits. Many of us simply eat too much. For others, the problem lies in the quality of nourishment. Food that has been refined and devitalised has had many nutrients drained from it. Your being responds to the love in the food you eat.

Addictions besides food and substances. There are many other addictions, such as sex, overstimulation, crises, and depression.

Addiction to alcohol and other drugs, a highly prevalent phenomenon, is beyond the scope of this book. If you suspect it is an energy leak in your life, try eliminating the offending drug for one month. You will know without question. If you find a sizeable resistance to doing this, there is a good chance you have a problem, in which case outside help may be called for. If your partner has a problem, we recommend getting help of your own, perhaps through an organisation such as Al-anon.

Addictions put us out of touch with our natural feedback mechanisms. For example, if you are addicted to caffeine, you will interpret the feeling of tiredness, actually a cry for rest, as signalling a need for more caffeine, which further depletes the body's energy reserves. Further, with caffeine you get used to a much higher level of tension in the nervous system, which becomes your normal way of feeling. Many households, not realising the role caffeine can play in the emotional climate, have become accustomed to low-level irritability as a standard background hum.

It's interesting to note the connection between caffeine and alcohol. Regular use of caffeine strains the nervous system, and by the later part of the day you crave to soften the harsh edges of that stress. Alcohol is one way of accomplishing this, since for some it does balance out the irritability. If you like alcohol, caffeine may increase your craving for that drug. The next day, as a result of the alcohol, the system is further dulled and depleted and desires yet more caffeine to stay alert. This in turn gives rise to yet more craving for alcohol. For some people, in place of caffeine substitute sugar, which has many of the same reactions. Many are caught up in this cycle.

A major addiction is TV. Activities such as watching TV are not necessarily in themselves energy leaks; the problem is the misuse of entertainment. There is no harm if you consciously balance out your focused intensity by relaxing into a detective story, a TV programme or a movie. But if you use TV to avoid, then you may have a serious energy leak.

Lack of rest and sufficient high quality sleep is a highly prevelant energy leak. What makes it difficult to recognise is that a low-to-moderate deprivation of rest or sleep does not always show up as tiredness. Instead the symptoms are often similar to excess caffeine or sugar: irritability, depression, or a ragged nervous system. We become so used to these symptoms that we do not suspect they might be signalling need for change. For many, just a few days of deep rest would bring a surprising change in the nervous system. For others, an hour or two more sleep each night might bring back a peace they had long forgotten.

Not expressing your feelings. Unexpressed feelings have a habit of turning in on themselves. They become disease, depression, fatigue, hostility, sexual shutdown, passive-aggressive behaviour, or emotional paralysis.

Stressful relationships represent one of the most powerful and prevalent energy leaks. We hope this book will be of help in dealing with this one.

Not doing in your daily life what you love. Were we not designed to get up in the morning with passion for what the day brings? The notion of work has a very strange feeling, so antithetical to the natural rhythms of life. So many of us accept long hours doing what we do not really care for. And when we are not working, we often spend insufficient time doing things that truly nourish us. How many, were they to step back from their life and take a broader look, would find they are no longer living according to their truest priorities?

If life has lost its passion, perhaps your spirit is asking you to rediscover your true needs. If you take time to renew your spirit you will be better able to distinguish your true needs from the counterfeit ones. What you did not truly want will never satisfy in any quantity.

We feel it is especially important for women to find ways of nourishing themselves outside their relationship (this does not mean sexually!). By so doing they help dissolve the traditional female resentment that stems from perpetually giving. In addition, by finding something of value outside the relationship they will put less pressure on their partners and feel less dependant on them. It is not selfish to make time for what truly replenishes your spirit. On the contrary, it is an act of rejuvenation that liberates you to more effective action.

Lack of proper exercise. At each moment the body contributes far more than we realise to the totality of how we are feeling. Many of us get used to a body that feels deadened, not realising how very much it affects the quality of our consciousness. When the body lacks vitality we become dull without realising it.

Lack of exercise, like other energy leaks, can be a self-perpet-uating habit. Feeling uncomfortable with a sluggish body, one attempts to escape through various forms of bodily indulgences, which, after initial relief, leave the system yet more unbalanced and drained. Now, with a greater discomfort level, the depleted system finds exercise increasingly distasteful. To complete the vicious circle, the lack of exercise further contributes to a depressed state, encouraging further unhealthy activity.

To break out of this arduous cycle, think of pushing a car that has broken down. A great burst of energy is required to get it going, but once the car is moving, a much lighter push will keep it moving. Breaking free of sloth is similar.

If you wish to step out of the prison of dullness, bring your physical energy more to life. Stretch, dance, loosen and free your body, so you can more fully liberate the vitality of life within you. Just as you cannot easily play beautiful music through a clogged instrument, it is difficult to feel joy when your body has needs which have too long gone dishonoured.

Lack of sufficient contact with nature. It is useful to recognise the feeling of being indoors too much. For us it is a musty, stuffy feeling in the mind, a bit like being in a dank, ill-lit prison. Its symptoms are easily relieved by going outdoors away from the clamour. Nothing brings balance and perspective more quickly to a troubled heart than allowing the harmony of nature to enter and heal.

Lack of time spent alone. We bring so much more to our intimacies when we take a balanced amount of time alone. A by-product of addiction to activity is our perpetual work and play with oth-ers, neglecting our solitude. Many of us in the modern world get swept up into a life which seems to have its own momentum of nervous, agitated energy. The end product is a profound imbalance in which a major source of nourishment has dried up. Drinking at the fountain of silence occurs most often when one is alone.

Resistance in general is a fundamental energy leak. It freezes

167

energy that could otherwise be in circulation, taking away from our basic aliveness. Discomfort in daily life arises far more from our resistance than from the circumstances we are resisting.

The phenomenon takes many forms, but they all have in common a sense that things should be other than what they are. This leads to a tightening of mind and body. The feeling is often accompanied by an anxious effort to control, along with the fear that the future won't unroll the way we wish. We resist our partner's behaviour, the state of our health, our moods and feelings, our financial fortunes, and in general whenever things don't go the way we prefer. Learning to accept is a major theme of many great spiritual teachings, especially from the East.

Poor Breathing. Emotions and breathing have an interesting relationship to one another. Positive emotions are associated with deep, regular, slower breathing; negative with shallow, irregular, faster breathing. When your emotions change, your breathing is affected.

But especially important to those who would transmute their energy, it works equally the other way. Changing your breathing has a significant effect on your emotions. The first way to change your breathing is simply to become aware of it. The second is to soften your diaphragm.

Breathing associated with feelings of freedom, peace, and joy has as a predominant feature a soft belly, relaxed diaphragm, belly expanding on inhale, chest remaining relatively steady. Try consciously breathing in this fashion, sitting or lying for a few minutes, doing nothing but being aware of your breath. You may find it harder for difficult feelings to persist in this new environment. Experiment with it and you will come to appreciate the powerful effect conscious breathing can have on your emotional state.

Lack of touch. The need to be touched is most obvious in the young of humans and other animals, but it is equally true for the rest of us. Lack of touch is much like lack of a basic nutrient.

For touch to be nourishing it needs to be loving and

conscious. Sexual touch can be this, although often it isn't. Massage is an excellent way of learning to give this fine gift. Even five or ten minutes on the head, neck, shoulders, feet, back, buttocks, or any other place that calls for attention, can fill an extremely important gap.

Incidentally, many older people cease to receive touch, much to their detriment. Learning the value of touch now may help you and your partner continue enjoying it as you get older. *The thought process.* This is the ultimate energy leak, so much part of us, as the ocean this fish swims in, that it may not be seen as anything special. But as we have seen from the preceding chapter, a great wastage of energy occurs from fearful thinking.

ELIMINATING ENERGY LEAKS

In addition to increasing and harmonising your energy, taking care of energy leaks will also nourish the spiritual side of your intimacy by creating conditions for greater awareness in your interractions.

The way you start the day can set the tone for your level of consciousness. The tradition of pouring a cup of coffee first thing and sinking into the newspaper leads in one direction. Another way is to start the day by reading something together from a book that reminds you of what perspectives you would like to carry with you through your day. Meditating together, even if for a short while, is another way of encouraging conscious priorities. The conclusion of your day also deserves attention, for it determines the kind of energy you carry into your sleep.

Take time every day to allow the agitation of daily life to settle. It helps to meditate, or do yoga, or any discipline which balances and harmonises your energy. Share your common interest in becoming more conscious, or more loving. Talk about your successes as well as your struggles, and acknowledge each

other for the work you have been doing. Open yourself together-
er frequently to whatever your deeper wisdom would have you
know on your path.

Stay in touch with nature on a regular basis, and if possible
take frequent walks in beautiful places together. Keep the body
sensitive in whatever way you can. Tack up reminders in your
home. It helps to form alliances with others who are also trying
to awaken. Meet with other couples who are trying to be conscious. Remind each other lovingly of what is important and
what isn't. Support and encourage each other in activities that
foster greater aliveness and awareness.

One activity in particular has been a great blessing for Martha
and I in nurturing sensitivity of mind and body for the past twen-
ty-six years. Shortly before meeting Martha, I had discovered
hatha, or physical, yoga, and I shared it with her. At thirty-two
I was beginning to feel the first signs of ageing. Here was something that I could tell would have a profound effect upon the
way the body aged. Within a few short weeks of starting yoga I
could already begin to feel a notable difference in the way my
body felt and moved.

The feeling is difficult to put into words, for I had never felt it
before. I felt younger, but without the often nervous energy of
youth. I felt more like an animal, a wild one moving with more
grace. I breathed deeper, slower. My posture became naturally
more erect. I felt more alert and energised, yet more relaxed. When
I sat down an instant tranquility would often come over me.

Besides transforming the way I felt, yoga also taught me an
important lesson about how to respond to tightness, whether it be
physical or mental. Traditionally one either does battle with tightness or ignores it. Neither is effective. To fight against tightness is
resistance, which only serves to increase it. Ignoring it is an equally
inadequate response, since tightness is a message from the system to
do something.

Without appropriate response to tightness the body ages
without grace. Most people stay away from the tight areas of

their body, the places where the muscles are becoming unnaturally rigid. As a result the body begins to close in on itself. The range of movement becomes increasingly limited, the tissues tighten up with age, and there is a resultant diminution of energy flow to the various organs, bringing slow atrophy. We are led to believe this is normal ageing.

Yoga showed me what it means to avoid both battling tightness and ignoring it. The third alternative is to play with it consciously. Shortly after beginning to practice yoga I learned about its essence, which involves playing the edge.

The edge is a degree of stretch that lies between comfort on one hand and pain on the other. When stretching brings pain, one has gone beyond the edge. The postures are highly refined tools for exploring the nature of limit in the body and, in so doing, opening up long-held areas of tightness.

Yoga is a deep leverage for change. A major aspect to yoga is exploring the nature of blocked energy. As the body ages, it tightens around the nerves, glands, circulatory system and tissues. Yoga allows one to come into direct contact with the nature of resistance in the body, so that one can actually feel the blocks. This allows the body to begin breaking out of confining patterns, through intimate and subtle ways of working directly with these blocks. By repeatedly going to the edge and staying there, the edge begins to move in the direction of opening the body.

Postures which appeared impossible to me yielded over time to an almost miraculous loosening of the tissue. The edges moved further and further back without any effort on my part, although I did allow myself to linger as consciously as possible in places of intensity. I came to see that the quality of yoga depended not on how flexible one was, but rather on the quality of attention they brought to playing their edge.

Playing the edge involves finding a creative balance between the polarities of control and surrender, safety and adventure. The capacity for focused attention is refined. Using one's own body as a teacher, one changes the relationship with

171

their body so they are no longer alienated from it. The body can actually become more finely tuned as it ages.

Over time I have found that edges go well beyond the physical. Hatha yoga is like entering the narrow end of a funnel that begins to widen into unsuspected areas of life.

DISCIPLINE AND FREEDOM

The word 'discipline' has been often used to mean the attempt to force yourself to do something you would rather not be doing. But discipline can have a very different meaning in an adult life, one that is essential to learning.

One part of us longs for the quiet, pristine order of the life of spirit. It does not want to be a victim of cravings, driven by compulsions that are not really in our best interest. Another part longs for the passionate encounter available through the life of the senses, and does not want to destroy our passion through some ruthless ascetic measures. This aspect of us wants to satisfy desires in the moment, whenever and wherever they occur. We're feeling a bit down, so we light a cigarette, or pour a drink, or head for the refrigerator. It's easy, and for the moment it works.

There is no reason, really, why we shouldn't do whatever we feel like in the moment. But following the consequences alertly over time will show clearly where different desires lead, and what kind of experiences they produce. Some cravings lead to energy leaks, others to greater harmony.

Allowing ourselves to succumb to immediate gratification whenever we want seems superficially to bring us freedom. But in fact the reverse is true. Doing whatever we desire in the moment makes us a veritable slave to our cravings.

Seeing this, my deeper wisdom may decide that life would be more interesting and healthy were I to eliminate certain unwholesome habits. But were I to indulge myself in the so-called freedom to do whatever I want, whenever I want it, then my capacity to say no to life-denying habits is lost to me. In fact I am caught in a rather limited sphere of behaviour. Therefore true freedom requires discipline. It lies in having the capacity, in the interest of a greater good, to say no to the behaviours that no longer serve me.

The capacity for discipline becomes essential when your deeper wisdom urges you to explore what it would be like to eliminate an energy leak. The same universal force that urges every being towards greater aliveness and creativity is now urging you to stop doing the things that, while they bring immediate gratification, actually cause you to become deadened and mechanical. True discipline is not the forbidding of any particular behaviour, but the capacity to listen your deeper wisdom for guidance.

Identify the biggest energy leak in your life, whether it's food, drugs, lack of exercise, too much activity or mindless entertainment, undealt-with feelings, or whatever. Changing just that one thing often begins a chain reaction that spreads into every area of your life.

A real magic is possible when a couple explores what it would be like to get rid of energy leaks. Any kind of a discipline you make with your partner will bring more consciousness into your lives. To have a discipline together makes it more enjoyable in the light of the mutual support. Together you can create structures which eliminate or lessen some of the more energy-draining aspects of your life. If you are not sure where to begin, just take a few moments together and go within, asking your deeper wisdom which areas of your life would benefit from change. With attention to your energy leaks, the feeling in your home can undergo a major transformation in a surprisingly short time.

chapter 10

FEAR

Most people who observe themselves with any honesty will perceive fundamental aspects of themselves with which they are not comfortable and want to change. Those who attempt this change will inevitably find major obstacles. For change to occur it is necessary to be intimate with these obstacles and respectful of their strength. Where are these obstacles to be found?

Our own personal set of obstacles can be found at a certain layer of our mind. To find these barriers, we divide our consciousness into three levels. The outer level is our superficial personality, our conditioned mind, caught in the dream and laced with fear, but often claiming it wants peace and love. The deep layer in the heart of our being shines brightly with our true nature, which is nothing but love. The real challenge lies in the middle layer, the great obstacle to change. Therein dwell the more elusive layers of our darkness, the intense core of our painful dream, our forgetting. Here are found the hidden and twisted threads of fear and guilt, which have an energy and influence greater than the outer layer. Because the middle layer

174

is not conscious under normal circumstances, it is more insidious in blocking us from the direct experience of our innermost core. For any real change in our life to happen, we must take this unconscious layer seriously into account. As long as it isn't dealt with, we make a prison of it.

Gurdjieff, the enigmatic Russian spirtual teacher, once said the single most important step in getting out of prison is first to recognise that you are in prison. Our prison is whatever keeps us from feeling the birthright of love and joy. We call it the ego. We are not using the word here in the technical sense of Freudian psychotherapy. Rather, we are employing it to stand for a part of the mind that we have created. It believes itself separate and cut off from the whole and is therefore afraid and incapable of love. One highly important step in attaining freedom lies in learning to recognise when we are caught in one of its many forms.

The ego is a belief about who we are, arising out of an elemental misperception. Somewhere along the way the mind came to the conclusion that it was separate from the whole, as if a wave believed itself separate from the ocean. From this single thought has emerged the entire world as we perceive it. Ego, the seemingly separate entity, lies at its centre. In this perception my self appears to be a body, cut off from other selves and isolated from the source of all life. This ego, like everything in the world of form, faces the certainty sooner or later of ceasing to exist. The wave, in forgetting it is part of the ocean, fears breaking on shore as an ultimate catastrophe.

Ego is the source of all the conflict and pain in our relationship, for it does not coexist with love. When ego is present, fear is the basis of consciousness and there are problems. When love is present, there may be challenges and obstacles, but without fear there are no problems. In a way this greatly simplifies things. Two partners, instead of confronting a great variety of problems in their intimacy, now address a single challenge. Of course ego seems a formidable challenge, since it is so deeply rooted, persistent and frequently intense.

Wherever ego is found, fear lurks. Since ego is terrified of coming to an end, fear pervades its activities. Most of our current responses to fear breed more fear. Release from this entanglement entails learning a different response to fear.

FEAR HAS MANY FORMS

Fear is part of the human journey, just as winter and darkness are part of the cycles of nature. It presents a precious opportunity to mature into one's full intelligence.

Nothing affects the quality of my life more significantly than the way I respond to fear. It displays itself incessantly in many forms throughout the day as I relate with my partner, read the newspapers and watch TV, relate with others, and especially as I encounter the chatter of my own mind.

Fear is a single tree with many branches: boredom, dullness, depression, illness, anxiety, pain, hurt, anger, blame, guilt, conflict, violence, worry. No matter how far removed a distant branch extends from the trunk of this tree, it will always partake of the essential quality of fear, which is an unhealthy tightening of mind and body, preventing the awareness of love. Whenever love appears absent you can be sure that fear is present.

If things are going badly, fear announces that they will never get better. The pain I'm feeling now will never go away, and it's hopeless. If things are going well, fear reminds you that it won't last, things will get worse. I'll lose my health, my relationship, my money, my job, my good mood. Fear makes sure you never win.

FEAR AS OUR TEACHER

Lurking a few inches under the surface, fear waits to spring. It enters in the dark and invites us convincingly to listen to its promises of keeping us safe. Although it goes against all reason for fear to keep us safe, we believe its promises. We carry layers of armouring in our muscles because we feel the need for protection. In the mind we worry obsessively, we cling to the past, we try to control the uncontrollable future, we resist the present, seeking in vain to find a sense of security. We also erect defences for our seeming safety at the emotional level, by closing the heart. The very mechanism which exists in order to 'protect' us serves to keep us from the awareness of love.

Day and night, the overheated mind remains in a state of continual stress, contracted against the threat perceived in virtually everything. The apprehension of danger lurks in the behaviour of our partner, in someone being unkind to us, in the prospect of getting older, in our work, our pleasure, our finances, our body. But no matter how adroitly we juggle our images, the threat feels unrelenting.

We have taken on the habit of listening to fear as our teacher because it promises us something we desperately want. In myths the devil is attractive, smart and believable. Fear is wily and knows how to sound terribly reasonable.

When the body is in genuine danger, fear plays a useful role as a cry to pay close attention or to take immediate action. But other than physical danger, do we really have anything to fear? Either psychological fear is real and justified, or it's an interpretation based on an illusion.

Walking at twilight I see a rope and confuse it for a rattlesnake. Although my fear is quite palpably real, it exists because of a mistake. I am afraid, but not actually in danger. We wish to find out if the vast majority of our fear is of this nature.

SCEPTICISM AND FAITH

Despite the fact that the intellect has lately been given a bad reputation in some spiritual circles, it can be a vital tool in the great task of confronting fear. The mind normally tends to serve and perpetuate fear by its unquestioning faith in the reality of things as they seem to be. I think it would help if we were more sceptical.

Scepticism has a place in the service of spirit. It asks us to challenge our most cherished beliefs, particularly the ones that imply danger. It says, there is advantage in being more distrustful of the seemingly obvious premises of fear, so deeply ingrained in the human consciousness. If we sense the importance and truth of this, a vigilance arises in which we become suspicious every time fear tells us that we need to defend, blame, or worry.

Although seeming opposites, scepticism and faith are joined at the core. There are two major belief systems about the essence of life, one believing we are in danger and the other that we are safe. To be sceptical of one is to have faith in the other. Even those who see themselves as having no faith in fact have a great deal of faith. The traditional, conditioned mind, sceptical of the notion that we are in fact safe, has faith in the 'obvious'. It believes that things are as they seem, that the universe is an unsafe place, that all the defences of fear are necessary to remain secure. Our own fear level is proof of our faith in this belief.

In the awakening mind things are reversed, for it is highly sceptical of the obvious. It challenges the notion that we are a body, doomed to die, in danger everywhere, and in continual need to defend ourselves. The awakening mind has glimpses of its true safety. If some of the light shining deep within manages to filter through the thick clouds of forgetting into our conscious awareness, we call it faith. The faith of the awakening mind is also expressed as scepticism towards the perception of psychological danger.

Perhaps the ego's central belief is that I am not safe. When I envision relationship as a spiritual path, I am asking to use every difficult situation to help illuminate this crucial issue. Since intimacy is a particularly fertile field for perceiving danger, I am given endless opportunities to challenge this belief. Whenever I get upset at my partner, whenever I withdraw, I have a fine opportunity to explore my feeling of being threatened. I might typically feel threatened when my partner frowns at me, or withdraws from me, or uses a certain tone of voice, or gets angry at me, or isn't in tune with me sexually, or doesn't remember to keep agreements, or seems unsupportive, or fails to hear my truth, and so on. This convincing fear casts its shadow over my inner world, insisting firmly that it isn't safe to love.

Here is the question continually confronted by the spiritually orientated relationship: is the threat actually genuine? If we were truly threatened, fear, with all its protective defences, would be an appropriate response. But if the feeling of threat is based on a false belief, then we are thinking like a classic paranoid, who is frightened when in fact no threat exists, except in his mind.

One way of defining the work of a spiritual relationship is to explore together the radical notion that, in fact, no threat does exist.

GREETING FEAR LOVINGLY

If the feeling of threat is but an interpretation, there is an alternative way of perceiving. Fear's voice is not the only available teacher.

Although I may not be able to prevent fear from arising in my mind, I do have a choice of whether or not I accept it as my teacher. There is another teacher within, which we call the voice of loving truth, or the deeper wisdom. Never far from my awareness, its quiet voice remains largely unheard around the clamorous static of the fearful mind. This other teacher lets me know, any time I stop to ask, that I am now and have always been safe. But if I am entrenched in the habit of believing fear, I seldom ask myself what love is saying right now.

The voice of love is available even to a mind with a fearful content. The content is the changing flow of outer and inner events. The sun is shining, there is the sound of a bird in the distance, there is a pain in the knee, a feeling of low energy, a thought about food, and a vague feeling of sadness. All this is content.

Each moment of my life I have a choice of the way I hold the content, my fundamental posture towards it. I call this attitude the context. I can greet the content with a fundamental no as context, believing in fear and resisting the content. I also have the opportunity to say yes as context, embracing the content with love. This is especially useful whenever I am confronted with fear as content. I neither deny nor repress the fear, but hold it with an embracing yes. What does this feel like in practice?

If you are aware of fear, first feel it in its purity, abandoning the thoughts that normally accompany it. Breathe deeply with a soft belly for a few breaths. Then soften around the fear, the same way you might soften your muscles around a hypodermic needle to change the experience of pain into mere sensation. This is a mental softening, as if you were surrounding the fear in love. Each moment of life, each now, you have a fresh opportunity to choose love, to bring the light where darkness was, to open the heart where the heart had been closed. Choosing love is a simple gesture, ever available, always the same regardless of the content.

It is a continual challenge to recognise fear in all its guises. A distinctive feeling occurs whenever fear seeks a place in the mind where it can take root and multiply itself. It is helpful to recognise this feeling in your body, in your thinking, in your heart, as quickly as it arises. Realise this is the same voice of fear that you have been believing all your life. Fear is a very poor teacher. Look where listening to it has brought us all. Consider refusing its teachings and listening to a different teacher.

Fear is cagey enough to masquerade as love, a frequent occurence. However fear can always be recognised by its mode of operation, for even disguised as love, fear resists and fights, blames and judges. Fear also thrives when I reason with it and even when I fight against it, for to do either is still to accept its premise that danger is real, and therefore to encourage more fear. To meet fear at its own level is the biggest mistake.

Love does not resist, having no need to fight against fear, any more than light has to fight against darkness. Love simply shines forth, dissolving fear in its light. Love embraces the whole content of experience, pleasant or painful. Such a love lives in a plane beyond the dualism of good and bad, neither clinging to the former nor resisting the latter.

Each moment that I encounter fear I am granted the freedom to respond with yes or no. When I say yes, I am willing for this moment to be whatever it is. I am willing for my partner to have their fear or anger. I am willing for them to show me no love. I am willing to allow my contracted feelings in response to that. I am willing for my reaction to my partner's behaviour to be imperfect. I am willing to trust the process which led us to this point. My willingness to say yes to this moment is the voice of love in action.

The moment and place where I make the decision to choose either fear or love is usually unconscious. However, I cannot alter my decision unless I am aware of making it. Therefore, in learning to choose love, I need to learn how to be conscious of the moment and place where I make my decision.

I once became aware of such a moment when I slipped on the ice and landed uncomfortably and very ungracefully, with the wind knocked out of me. There was a moment's pause, and then I burst unexpectedly into laughter at my clumsy plunge. Just prior to the laughter, I remembered a split second of choice, a moment of truth, where I saw how I could either get really upset or laugh. I am aware of making a choice during that instant, one that felt somehow healthier.

I wish to develop this awareness more globally. The instant before I get upset with my partner I make such a choice, probably unconsciously. I want to become aware of making that choice, so that I can make a different choice. I want to learn better what I am growing to suspect: at bottom it is all my choice. I want to make use of as many negative moments as possible to practice seeing where and how I make the choice, and choosing again. I will receive many opportunities, particularly with my partner.

Words can only go so far in describing the inner gesture of making the other choice, and saying yes to fear. By practicing this gesture I may find that the quality of my negative experiences changes, sometimes dramatically. Whenever I greet fear with love, that very love becomes my reality. Every time I consciously lift from the battleground I learn afresh that the way out of conflict is instantaneous.

By making this gesture as often as needed, I begin to suspect that the entire thought system by which I have led my life is untrue to its very core. Fear is a false teacher. To ward off fear I have put great energy into striving for security, pleasure or power. Clearly none of these has brought me what I truly want, and never will. It becomes increasingly evident that only love will bring the satisfaction I crave.

A powerful force is set in motion when a couple unites to confront fear head-on. Realising that they have been listening for a lifetime to the voice of fear, they now combine their wisdom, reminding themselves as often as possible to listen to the voice of love. Whoever is more conscious can take the lead.

THE REAL SOURCE OF DISCOMFORT

While living in Alaska I once bought 80 acres of semi-remote land with a friend. We hastily erected a six-by-nine foot sauna, in which we spent the intense, frigid, largely dark Fairbanks winter while we were building a larger cabin. It was quite an experience in intimacy!

One morning I awoke bathed in sweat, uncomfortably roasting in the overheated room. I complained to my friend, who was fiddling with the wood stove, 'Findlay, for God's sake turn the stove down and open the door. It's awful in here, it must be at least 95 degrees!'

Findlay turned to me and calmly announced that he had thought to start the morning with a sauna. Then a strange thing happened. All of a sudden the heat, which was getting more intense by the moment, totally lost its uncomfortable quality and transformed magically into the friendly warmth of a sauna.

I was impressed by this event, and thought about it for a long time afterwards. The same physical sensation of intense heat was experienced first as a sticky-hot, undesirable intrusion, and then suddenly as a warm, friendly sensation. If you had initially asked me about the source of my discomfort, I would have had no doubt that it lay in the physical sensation of too much heat. Yet a moment later the word sauna served to trigger a powerful change in my experience. Since sauna stood for something desirable, the symbol allowed me to let go of my resistance to the heat. Suddenly I had given myself permission to enjoy what I had previously hated.

There was no room for doubt. The source of my discomfort was not, as I had assumed, the simple experience of heat. Rather, it lay in the mind through which the experience got interpreted. A simple shift in perspective and discomfort became comfort.

Whenever we are disturbed we usually believe our feeling was created by circumstances. In intimacy we traditionally accept that we are upset because of our partner's imperfections. But a major shift occurs when we begin to challenge the source of our feelings.

We are not upset for the reasons we think. Our belief says that we are troubled with our partner because of the fact that they spoke angrily to us and accused us of something we did not do. In truth, we are upset from our interpretation of our partner's actions. Through the filter of our conditioned mind, we interpret that our partner's unfair anger at us means we are unsafe.

When such fear arises, its discomfort may be the universe's way of suggesting that we are now seeing through a distorted lens. Our uneasiness is inviting us to challenge the inner posture with which we have greeted the disturbing event.

Our moments of upset, under the seemingly disparate surface fluctuations, have a monotonous similarity. He did that, she said this, which means I am unsafe. So when my partner says something critical, or looks at me a certain way, or uses a particular tone of voice, or does not listen, or does not accept me the way I am, or is not emotionally present, or is sexually insensitive, I have interpreted that to mean I am in danger.

I know I am making such an interpretation by the contracted feeling in my body and a loss of energy. I know from the black thoughts in my mind, the way I blame my partner and close my heart to them, my defensiveness, or the way I feel hurt and rejected. None of these reactions is possible when I am feeling truly safe.

I have often, when the person at the check-out counter scowled at me, left the shop feeling a little bit worse than before. When someone seemed unsupportive, I had determined that my being was threatened. In clear moments I perceive that interpretation is a mistake on the part of a confused mind. It is becoming plain that 99.9% of the pain and discomfort I feel in my adult life results from similarly mistaken interpretations. My feeling of continual threat exists in the absence of any real danger. The same is true for my partner.

Perhaps this is why, in walking down the street, you do not see very many adults who seem to be enjoying themselves. Most of us move through our lives more or less continually over-stressed. We feel tension not only from the pressure of having to get things done, but even more from our fearful interpretation of the events in our life, including the behaviour of our partner.

Whenever Martha and I investigate our own negativity we are always led to the truth – that things are not what they seem to be. The mind is mistaken both in believing that we are unsafe and that our pain is caused externally. Neither my partner nor events cause my suffering. It is caused by my mind alone and more specifically by that part of my mind I call my ego.

IS THE EGO REAL?

This ego, which plays such a dominant role in the life of the relationship, seems so dense, so solid, so very real. It might seem strange to ask whether the ego is in fact a reality. Nevertheless, the continual challenging of the ego's reality serves to erode its hold. Moments of clarity may appear, glimpses of truth that show us the ego has the same reality as a child's nightmare. It is very real to the child when it's happening, yet without the slightest substance to it.

What would it mean in practical life if the ego were not real? We respond to something that isn't real in a very different way from our response to what has reality. Think of the countless times you may have reacted to your partner's ego with attack and defence, as if you were genuinely threatened. But if ego is not real you can't be threatened and require no defence.

In every fearful occasion lies an opportunity to uncover and then challenge the belief that ego is real. And if your ego is not real, there is no need to be hard on yourself for seeming to have one. If it has no reality, it can be no bigger, smaller, better or worse than anyone else's, though it is in the nature of the ego to condemn itself and other egos. The most shameful places are remarkably similar in everyone.

What causes the mind to conceive such a strange notion that the ego is not real? Some of the practices we have discussed in this book can give a clue. If you do open-hearted listening with persistance you will begin to have an experience where you are able to step out of the ego by a peculiar kind of inner gesture. When you let go of the ego it is not vanquished, like a deadly enemy. It simply isn't there, just as darkness simply isn't there when light comes. The light of love, always present at your core, is available to shine away the darkness of ego.

After frequently observing that which seemed so very dense and solid to evaporate in one instant, you may begin to sense with growing assurance that the ego is darkness that disappears in the light of love. The ego is a dream that ends in the moment of awakening, offered by life every moment of now.

True intimacy cannot exist between one ego and another, but it can take place when two people are interested in waking up from the dream. Every time our partner relates to us from their ego we have an opportunity to practice stepping out of our own ego by seeing theirs as not real. Therefore at such times our partner is giving us a gift, offering us the possibility to feel love again, by changing the way we regard them. We are not our egos.

The belief in the reality of ego has persisted for thousands of years, in part because it hasn't gone sufficiently challenged. Imagine the powerful force for change if both members of a couple were intent on challenging the reality of ego when it arose.

GETTING INTO THE DARKNESS TOGETHER

From an airplane you can observe that an east-flowing river, as it loops around, is actually flowing at various points north, south, east and west. If you are floating down the river, even though its basic direction is east, it's going to look some of the time as if you were going west.

Similarly, you can expect as intimacy increases that there will be times when the relationship feels as if it has regressed and seems to become more negative, more crazy, more intensely dark and uncomfortable than it has ever been. Your increased negativity can actually be a healthy sign, signalling the creation of sufficient safety and trust for your deeper layers of repressed fear, pain and anger to emerge.

During times of difficulty, whoever is the more conscious in the moment can act as the beacon, and in a healthy relationship it will switch back and forth. The one holding the light can remind the other that we have asked for pockets of unconsciousness and fear to come to the surface, to be seen compassionately for what they are and to be released. The more intense the negativity, the closer we are to the core of the illusion. Instead of using this situation to blame each other, let's use it to investigate what's really going on here.

As Martha's and my trust increased we went through periods lasting several weeks where our disharmony was more intense. It seemed as if every little thing could trigger immense anger. At times we thought something was terribly wrong and we felt literally insane. Our east-flowing river was looping west, displaying some challenging rapids. In the flow of our relationship there were also longer periods where the river was smooth and easy-flowing, and it was effortless to be loving.

We accepted this as a natural rhythm, because we now had the tools to respond effectively to the darkness. We could now resolve difficultes in minutes rather than days. Even while our egos were displaying themselves at their most raw and disturbing, we were able more often to love ourselves. In the midst of the most intense craziness we realised that we were eliminating our greatest inner toxins.

Martha and I have always kept in our heart the possibility that we could create a life together infused continually with the presence of love in our awareness. It may not be realistic at the present to expect that you uninterruptedly feel your love. But it is possible to become increasingly aware of fear's presence. And when you become conscious of fear, the next important step is to release your defences.

chapter 11

DEFENCES AND GUILT

THE MANY FORMS OF DEFENSIVENESS

ELIMINATING defensiveness is one of the great tasks of intimacy. Defensiveness prevents love and communication from flowing between the partners. Listening with an open heart can temporarily end defensiveness when something difficult is discussed. We now turn our attention in more detail to the cause of defensiveness and its transcendence.

You have possibly noticed that when your partner observes you critically, you tend to shut it out. Defensiveness is swift and automatic. It can be provoked not only by criticism, but by virtually any expression of fear, anger or pain from your partner. It can also be triggered by anything else your ego interprets as a threat. You may even respond defensively to your partner's happiness and success.

Because defensiveness takes many forms, it pays to become familiar with your own favourite versions. Defensivenss often takes the form of attack. We may also put up a thick wall, sulk, or withdraw. Many defend through denial. Others justify their behaviour. We may defend by inflating ourself with grandiosity.

Defence is often distraction, or not being fully present. We may discount our partner, sometimes with humour. Often we defend by moving from our true feelings into our intellect, analysing, lecturing, or arguing. Some partners will burst dramatically into anger or tears so they don't have to listen. Some defend by seeming to agree with their partner and then proceeding as usual. Whatever its form, defensiveness lies behind most failed attempts at communication.

Your body, if you pay attention, can be a useful source of information about the presence of defensiveness. Frequent physical indicators of defensiveness may include constricted breathing, contraction around your eyes and the muscles in your face, a tightness in the belly, abnormal posture, a brittle or higher-pitched quality in your voice, or raised shoulders.

Two Defensive Parents

Gina and Mark were an attractive young couple who were having repeated arguments, seemingly about the children. Gina had a real charge in her voice as she described how Mark favoured Seth, their older child, over Rachel.

'What really bothers me is you seem totally unaware of the effect you are having on Rachel. When you come into the room you smile at Seth, you pick him up, you treat him like he's the greatest thing in the world. In the meantime Rachel just sits there waiting for some love and she seldom gets very much from you. The poor thing probably thinks her father doesn't love her very much. I've asked you repeatedly to stop playing favourites and you just don't seem to get it! Last night I saw the same thing happen after you got home from work.'

Mark winced, and then shot back, 'Well, I'm not so crazy about the way you show the kids love. Your idea of love is to let them do whatever they want. From what I've seen you don't know how to say no to either of them. They just walk all over you. I was watching you yesterday when Rachel was taking so long to get dressed and you just wouldn't put your foot down. Kids need firmness, not a wishy-washy parent.'

Gina, who had actually been trying hard to be more firm, felt defensive that Mark, instead of acknowledging her efforts, often pounced whenever she slipped up. She had another level of annoyance in her voice as she responded:

'I'm not perfect, OK? But why can't you ever see my moments of success? It just infuriates me that you only notice what's wrong. You never recognise that I've been working as hard as I can to get a handle on discipline. Why can't you at least acknowledge my efforts?' She burst into tears.

Mark waited with a stony face for her to stop crying and said in a hurt tone, 'Well I feel exactly the same way! You've told me many times about what you saw as my favouritism and believe it or not, I've tried! I've been trying real hard to show more affection to Rachel and treat the kids more equally but you never seem to notice. All you do is jump on me when I forget. It feels like you become gleeful every time you see me make a mistake.'

Here is one of the most common grounds for marital discord. Gina and Mark each felt unacknowledged by their partner for trying to improve. Those who have worked hard to behave more consciously know how infuriating it can be when their partner notices only their failures and neglects to appreciate their moments of success.

To let go of their defences, Gina and Mark practiced listening with an open heart, where each one heard and validated the other's anger. Neither of them found great difficulty in validating the other's feelings, because each had experienced what it felt like not to be appreciated for the effort they were making to be a better parent. Feeling validated allowed them for the first time to release their defences.

Now Mark could say to Gina, 'I honestly see myself as working hard towards treating the children equally; but I'm sure there are times that I slip up. I give you permission to give me a signal if you think I'm being unfair and I promise to take an honest look at what I'm doing in the moment. And I'd love it if you were to acknowledge the work I've done in that direction.'

Gina thanked Mark with a smile, and responded, 'I know within myself the work that I have done to improve my limit-setting with the children. And I'm aware that I have a way to go. If you see me getting lax, I give you permission to let me know and I'll take a look at what's going on. And I truly believe that if you look closely you'll see that I am improving.' Mark appeared comfortable with that.

With their defences dissolved, Gina and Mark could take pleasure in acknowledging the work the other had done. At last they had become allies in bringing about what they both wanted, which was to give their children the very best.

THE SHELL OF PERSONALITY

Defences are not just responses to particular events. At a deeper level they manifest as an elaborate psychological structure, carefully honed since early childhood, with which we greet the world. When as young children we begin to individuate, a healthy and natural process, we also erect a psychological barrier. This wall of pretence arises from our belief that safety lies in being the way others wish us to behave. Here lies the core of our false personality, which inhibits true intimacy by covering over who we really are.

Most of what we present to the world and perceive of each other is this shell of personality. Various pictures may be painted on the shell, attractive or otherwise. In proportion to its thickness the shell prevents contact and intimacy. Encounters with other adults are so often unfulfilling because the exchange has occurred not between the two beings, but between the shells. Relationship is satisfying only when the shell is absent, and essences meet. The process of becoming intimate involves the dissolving of this personality shell. For this to occur we need to trace defensiveness to its ultimate source.

THE SOURCE OF DEFENSIVENESS

Defences occur only when you are feeling bad about yourself. When you are feeling good about yourself there is no need for defence. If someone criticises you in an area where you feel secure about yourself, check to see if you aren't free of defensiveness. You may examine what is said to see if it has any validity and if it does you have learned something of value. Defensiveness increases as you come upon self-doubt and unworthiness. The very area where you are most intent on proving your innocence may often be the place you feel the most guilty. The more you defend, the more you are convinced there is something wrong with you and the less safe you feel.

Your capacity for intimacy will depend on whether you accept these unwieldy defensive structures as a given necessity, or whether you challenge their very foundation. However, if you find that you are being defensive, there is no need for self-castigation. Instead, ask within if you are feeling bad about yourself and shift your attention lovingly to your inner state.

It is a blessing every time you are able to release yourself from the chronic need to explain, to prove yourself, to defend, because it does not bring the safety you are seeking. Sometimes it is best just to say, 'I am sorry, I blew it. I was unconscious and not aware of my impact upon you at that time. I was wrapped up in my own emotional reaction. Please forgive me.'

Your feeling of safety does not lie in more effective defences. Rather, it lies in seeing your absolute worthiness, which includes all of your imperfections. An innocent mind has no need of defences.

DEFENCES AND BOUNDARIES

When it is suggested that defences are not necessary, fear may rush in to tell us that without our defences we'll be a victim of our partner's behaviour, and they would walk all over us. Therefore, says fear, the only safety lies in keeping our defences vigilantly in place.

Everyone who has gone beyond the romantic stage of intimacy has to confront this paradox. On the one hand, the mind holds tightly to the seemingly reasonable belief that we can't survive without defences. On the other hand, it seems equally apparent that defences destroy intimacy. How can we remain safe and still have an intimate relationship? How can we open ourselves to another and still retain our full individual integrity? The answer lies in the distinction between defences and boundaries.

We all have likes, preferences and needs. From these arise the necessity to set healthy and appropriate boundaries with others as to what we will and won't tolerate. Loving and honouring ourselves will naturally give rise to such boundaries. Out of respect for myself, for example, I may not wish to remain long in the presence of someone who is trying to hurt me. In leaving I am making a loving boundary.

Defences, which are fear's way of trying to keep us safe, may superficially resemble loving boundaries, but they feel quite different. Defending means closing the heart in the interest of self-protection. Defences involve contraction, resistance, a diminution in the flow of life energy, a shutting down, a lessening of the feeling of love. They tend to trigger the same in our partner.

Unfortunately, we have learned since childhood to equate setting limits with closing the heart, having associated the need for boundaries with a great deal of anxiety. In addition, many of us seldom experienced loving boundaries when we were young. Therefore most people don't know how to make boundaries while keeping their heart open.

There are two common ways to miss the mark. Some, in order not to close their heart, avoid making clear boundaries. This gives the other undue power and leads to feeling like a victim of another's insensitive or inappropriate behaviour. Others make boundaries easily and close their hearts at the same time, which breeds another kind of resentment. For example, at the level of parenting the first mistake is the permissive parent, the second is the authoritarian parent. Of course, neither alternative is effectieve and neither feels good. It appears difficult to learn loving boundaries, the one alternative that feels good to the child and the adult.

Despite this difficulty, learning to make open-hearted boundaries is an ability necessary for intimacy. Some of us, in moments of skilful parenting, know what it feels like. It is worthwhile to explore together those areas in your relationship where loving boundaries might replace fear's defences. Resentment or anger are often indications that loving boundaries are needed. Discuss what loving boundaries might look like, sound like, feel like. Inquire together how you might gently remind each other that such boundaries are possible.

'I WANT MORE SPACE'

For many couples the boundary issue expresses itself in a particularly poignant fashion, where one person wants more contact, the other more space. Aaron and Shauna were such a couple. He valued his privacy. The only trouble was he frequently put up a barrier when Shauna wanted to be close. Shauna experienced this as a rejection, which made her feel bad about herself as well as upset with Aaron.

Aaron had a different view. He told us that he often felt pushed by Shauna into being closer than he wanted to be at the moment. He had difficulty, when he felt the need to be alone, presenting it to Shauna in a way that didn't hurt.

This is a common source of pain in intimacy. One reaches out for more contact, and the other, feeling overly demanded on, pulls back. Repeated quarrels and bad feelings are the frequent outcome. Is there a more conscious way of handling the situation?

One kind of desire in relationship centres on getting your own needs met. You want the other to be there for you, or to satisfy some personal craving, or you want them to leave you alone, and so on. But there is also a different kind of desire. Here you want the other to do what they want, you want them to be happy, you want them to have everything they need.

For the relationship to feel harmonious these two kinds of desires have to be in balance. If you have too much other-pleasing, you throw away your integrity by losing yourself in the other, and you'll likely end up resenting them. On the other hand, if you are without a sense of the other's needs living in you as part of your heart, then you miss out on the richness and joy of unconditional giving, and the fulfilment of your personal needs will feel rather empty. A successful relationship finds that equilibrium.

Aaron did not want Shauna to be the sole arbiter of when they were intimate. He wanted to be his own person and set his own limits. Such a desire for self-determination is perfectly healthy. But in being his own person Aaron has no need to put up defences, or push away his partner. He can be his own person within his relationship to her.

The way Aaron withdrew triggered Shauna into feeling like a frightened little girl. Perhaps it reminded her of when her mother or father were not emotionally available when she needed something important to her well-being. Of course that left an imprint. Aaron now has an opportunity to show his partner a level of respect that she has never before received, by making his boundaries with an open heart.

What kept Aaron from making gracious boundaries was guilt. When Shauna blamed him for not being available, he felt responsible for her pain and reacted with guilt. This caused him to pull back even more and he was even less able to help. She felt even more abandoned, pulled more intensely on him, and a classic vicious circle ensued.

This painful dynamic was interrupted when Aaron for the first time declined the temptation to feel guilty. Instead he remained comfortable with the fact that he was not as available as Shauna would like him to be, and even perhaps as he would like to have been. Now, feeling good about himself, Aaron gave a different response.

He told her that he was feeling withdrawn, and was not able to be present. He emphasised that he wasn't abandoning her in his heart or trying to hurt her, but simply needed alone time to commune with himself. He also made a point of letting her know that he valued her and would be back.

Freed from guilt, Aaron could now be responsible and fair in coming upon the right balance between his own and his partner's needs. Sometimes he was able to go off in peace, clear with his needs and able to relax into himself. Because his needs were being fulfilled, he found there were other occasions when something in Shauna called forth to him and he was surprised to find his urgency for solitude evaporating.

Shauna found Aaron's new response more reassuring. Now it was easier for her to locate courage underneath her fear of aloneness. At last she could begin to release the belief that her safety and worthiness required his willingness to relate. Whenever Aaron said no she saw that it was time to find within herself the affirmation of her being for which she had been looking outside. Because Shauna was now willing to allow Aaron the expression of his own personal need, something in him was able to trust her further. At last they were moving towards freedom.

UNWORTHINESS CASTS ITS SHADOW

Like Aaron and Shauna, most of us feel rather bad about ourselves. The consequences of this guilt are immense. Besides experiencing specific instances of guilt for having committed 'bad' acts, the mind is pervaded with a more general, all-encompassing feeling of unworthiness. This may manifest as feelings of inadequacy, self-doubt or self-hatred, failure or unfulfilment, inferiority, depression, or a general sense that one's life is steeped in sin. It often expresses itself as a powerful feeling of shame. Normal human feelings, such as sadness or loss, can become unbearable when laced with such guilt.

Those who feel unworthy don't respect themselves. They send forth the message, largely unconsciously, that they are not worthy of being honoured. Others receive the message, again unconsciously, believe it, and oblige by withholding respect. In fact, others will tend to offer you respect in proportion to how much you respect yourself. To the extent unworthiness is present it is difficult to give and receive love.

The feeling of unworthiness also darkens our lives through self-sabotage. Those who feel guilty tend to punish themselves through illness, depression, overeating, and overindulgence in drugs, through accident and injury, through sabotaging relationship, or through the creation of scarcity and discomfort.

Guilt is an extraordinarily pervasive phenomenon. The more relational difficulties I witness, the more convinced I am that a sense of unworthiness is the source of virtually all our relational problems.

LETTING OUR PARTNER DEFINE OUR WORTH

When you were little your sense of worth came naturally from your parents. Now that you are an adult, it would be interesting to ask yourself if you allow your sense of worth to be defined by others. Do you give your partner, your parents, your friend, your boss, or an outside teaching the power to define whether or not you are worthy?

Most of us do. If your partner or parent is critical, you may feel little, compressed into a small space, as if they were right. If you become defensive, that implies you believe there is something true in their accusation, worth defending against. In either case you give the other the power to define your worth.

Perhaps it's time to take back this power. Your response to unloving behaviour would be transformed if you knew for certain that the other's evaluation of your worth was irrelevant. If you felt truly good about yourself, another's harshness would be seen as their cry for help, stemming from their own feeling of unworthiness. Such attempts would elicit compassion rather than guilt.

It is essential that we learn to open our hearts to ourselves, to honour and respect ourselves in the midst of our humanness. Yet most of us seem quite far from that level of inner peace. Is there a path to knowing our basic worthiness?

UNSUCCESSFUL WAYS OF DISPELLING GUILT

Several common strategies for dispelling guilt do not work. Letting them go is a step towards compassion for oneself.

Creating Ideals

The first strategy for feeling better about ourselves is to create ideals which we believe will prove our worth if we live up to them. Ideals can include making money, or being successful at work or in the community; or being attractive, thin, youthful looking, in good health, or disciplined. They can include living up to spiritual dictates such as being loving, moral, or non-violent, having good thoughts and feelings, or doing good deeds. Many ideals can be found around our intimacy, such as having an exciting sex life, or having a happy partner.

Although we hope to lessen our feeling of unworthiness by

living up to these ideals, what actually happens is quite the reverse. The ideal is the should, which we hold up continually against what actually is, and find ourselves wanting. Every time we fail to live up to our ideals, our level of guilt increases. In fact, we are never able to satisfy these ideals for long. Even if we should for a moment, the mind swiftly re-establishes our unworthiness by setting fresh ideals beyond our capacity to achieve.

Many who have not succeeded in living up to their ideals think of themselves as a failure. What a merciless and painful label to give oneself.

Imagine having two children, one of whom is successful at school, popular, attractive, pleasing of personality and knows just where she is going. The other gets bad marks, is socially clumsy and unpopular, totally confused about the direction of his life, and has pimples. Could you not imagine loving the second one, in the midst of his confusion, just as much as the first? You would scarcely want to use the word failure to describe a lost and confused child. The very word comes from an unloving place in our being. Failure could actually be considered a secular term for sinner, for it carries the same judgemental connotation.

Living up to ideals cannot possibly succeed in eradicating primordial guilt. If we feel unworthy in the core of our being, no change at the level of mere behaviour can touch our guilt.

Eliciting Continuous Approval

Another method of trying to expel our feeling of unworthiness is to find a partner who will approve of us continually. We are actually asking for the unconditional and continuous positive regard that we needed and did not get from our parents when we were infants. The worse we feel about ourselves the more we demand that our partner disagree with our self-evaluation and show us nothing but love. They are not allowed to be human and display their own childhood wounds. This strategy leads into a morass, for love must be freely given. Those who are with someone demanding to be continually loved, shut down. The more you demand to be loved to ease your feeling of unworthiness, the more you will blame your partner for not loving you enough and the more unloving both of you will become.

Feeling Superior

The third strategy is to find a person, or people, to whom you can feel superior. Your ego hopes that by finding others lacking you will establish your greater moral excellence, and thus be rid of inadequacy.

It is often your partner whom you elect to play this role. Many people complain about their relationship, attributing its failure to the insufficiencies of their partner. But the connection between blaming your partner for the quality of the relationship and your own feeling of inadequacy may not be apparent.

Because judging your partner seems to soften the pain of feeling unworthy, your mind may become quite vigilant and skilful in noticing their errors. Yet such a talent does not serve. Although judging brings a crude pleasure at the surface, at the depths it brings no satisfaction. Like drinking salt water to quench your thirst, the more you judge, the more unloving you become and the worse you feel about yourself. The burden of guilt is lightened by being vigilant instead towards releasing judgements of yourself and your partner.

If these common attempts to release guilt are destined to fail, we are interested to find what does help. A clue is found in exploring two very different inner voices.

GUILT AND CONSCIENCE

Learning to walk necessitates falling down, a natural part of the process. Learning to mature also requires falling down a great many times. A sense of peace with oneself depends on one's attitude towards the inevitable falling.

One perspective regards these mistakes as unfortunate and

regrettable occurrences. With this outlook the awareness of your failings will elicit either guilt or denial. The voice of guilt asserts that without feeling really bad about myself when I erred, I would have no way of correcting my mistakes. Without guilt, it says, I would become immoral, drown in chaos, or repeat the same mistakes endlessly.

But another voice within offers a different perspective towards my failings (or fallings). This is the voice of conscience, which takes care of my mistakes in a far more compassionate and effective way. Guilt and conscience are both the voice of an inner teacher who attempts to guide me when I make mistakes. Conscience is often confused with guilt, and it can be challenging to discriminate between them.

The difference lies in the spirit from which these voices emanate. Guilt and conscience have entirely different qualities. Guilt, arising out of fear and confusion, attacks like a harsh parent: 'Dammit, you fool, look at you! There you go again!' Most of us have an inner parent that frequently talks to us that way.

As a child, when your parents blamed you harshly, you likely had little desire to please. You may well have repeated the undesired behaviour in the reactive spirit of getting even, or in not wanting to respond favourably to such an unkind voice. The same is true when your inner parent is harsh with you. When you are guilty you tend to repeat the unwanted behaviour. Although guilt tells you self-condemnation is necessary to keep you from the sin of making a mistake, the truth is quite the contrary. You are far more capable of releasing an undesired behaviour if you are first able to love yourself in the midst of it.

An entirely different inner guide is available, kind and effective. Conscience sees your imperfections as an invitation to loving attention. When you replace guilt with conscience, you are able to regard your failings with a clear, unflinching glance, uncontaminated with blame. Conscience kindly points out when you make a mistake, always with love and respect, and urges you to try differently next time. You may be left with a gentle feeling of remorse, perhaps a momentary sadness for having caused pain. The feeling is often accompanied by gratitude for having learned something valuable.

True conscience has nothing to do with obeying the transient customs of society. Rather, it is a recognition of moral rightness, arising from the same depths where truth and beauty are seen. Conscience, being grounded in truth, is ultimately loving. Because it is loving it actually succeeds, unlike guilt, in correcting mistakes.

BEING A LOVING PARENT TO MYSELF

Becoming a father helped me discover the quality of being loving while pointing out mistakes. When my young son was misbehaving, it was possible to see that his behaviour was a result of being in confusion or pain, a cry for help. The same fear-based behaviour in an adult might have triggered me to close my heart. It wasn't so hard to make the necessary firm boundaries to prevent him from destroying property and hurting himself or others. In the act of making these boundaries I found I could say no to his behaviour while at the same time saying yes to his being. He could still feel my love.

Within me, too, is a scared, confused little boy, who sulks, lashes out, or acts inappropriately. When I am behaving in ways that Martha doesn't like, it is usually the hurt little boy in me. He, too, needs a loving parent. The way I am when being a good parent, or friend, can be my model of how I wish to respond to my own mistakes. I can learn to open my heart to myself when I am socially ungraceful, when I overindulge, when I 'fail' at something, when I close my heart; when I disply the ten thousand imperfections that are part of learning to be fully human.

Whenever I feel genuine compassion for myself I have a

natural interest in bringing more harmony into every aspect of my life. I notice mistakes and correct them spontaneously. But I do so with honour and respect for the maker of the mistakes. And in so doing, I find that there is a far greater tendency not to repeat them. Children who are lovingly corrected will more likely want to please their parent.

MOVING OUT OF SELF-JUDGEMENT

To develop this quality of honour and respect for yourself requires going beyond some powerfully entrenched conditioning. It is not a simplistic process that you can learn from a few rudimentary exercises in self-esteem. It takes focused attention on a regular daily basis.

Each day brings many incidents which provide opportunities for you to turn against yourself. It happens very quickly. The harsh critic in you arises and takes over the mind so rapidly that you don't even know it has happened. All your efforts to escape seem to trap you more tightly.

The moment that you become aware you have been judging yourself is a great opportunity. It is relatively easy to love yourself when you are functioning well. But when you have done something you dislike you have a chance to alter the self-feeding cycle of negativity.

When you are about to enter the old pattern of judging yourself, you can say instead: 'Because I hurt my partner, ate too much, did a poor job parenting, or closed my heart ... I am presented with an opening for change. I could easily move into self-judgement in the usual way. But I know from my own experience the resultant pain, and how pointless and unnecessary it is; so I hereby choose not to do so.' You have stopped perceiving the voice of self-blame as the truth, but rather as the point-of-focus for your work on yourself.

Every time you have an occasion to belittle yourself, you have at that very same moment a choice not to do so, and instead to affirm your power to deal with all situations with love and respect for yourself. Every time you decline an opportunity to be harsh with yourself you deepen your connection to the spring of innocence at the centre of your being.

What happens when you find yourself forgetting and engaging in the old pattern of self-blame? Occasions will still remain when you turn against yourself, for the old life-denying patterns take time to undo. When you notice this has happened, you have brought the unconscious, automatic quality of self-blame to the light of awareness, where it may be dissolved. Vigilance and persistance are required to continue noticing whenever you are blaming yourself, and to unhook the sense of self from that quality of blame.

Feeling bad about feeling bad is the trap. You are not asked to be perfect. Instead, you break the chain by refraining from judging yourself further even though your self-esteem has faltered. There is no finer expression of self-love than to see with forgiveness when you are not loving and accepting yourself. Life gives us a gift that perhaps we have not yet fully appreciated, which is the permission to make as many mistakes as we need. In the value system dominated by guilt, mistakes are considered grounds for self-hate. But love warmly accepts our seeming imperfections and rejoices in the opportunities they provide.

Those who have truly accepted their own shortcomings have no reason to pass judgement on others. Every time you forgive yourself for not living up to the standards you have created for yourself, you are also forgiving every other human being who has displayed a similar failing. Feeling better about yourself will allow you to be more gracious towards your partner's imperfections. Now it will be easier to take another step towards releasing your judgements and opening your heart more fully to the one you have come here to love.

By accepting, we were able more often to love ourselves. In the midst of the most intense craziness we realised that we were eliminating our greatest inner toxins.

Martha and I have always kept in our heart the possibility
that we could create a life together infused continually with the
presence of love in our awareness. It may not be realistic at the
present to expect that you uninterruptedly feel your love. But it
is possible to become increasingly aware of fear's presence. And
when you become conscious of fear, the next important step is
to release your defences.

chapter 12

OPENING THE HEART: THE GREATEST CHALLENGE

IS JUDGEMENT NECESSARY?

A basic reality of unhappy intimacies is the judgement each party develops towards their partner. No relationship can flourish with such mutual harshness.

In moving though life it is necessary to make many evaluations: being here would serve me better than being there, this food is not good for my body, this car is not good for my wallet. We call this discrimination, an essential quality for living in the world.

Judgement is something quite different, and involves the closing of our heart. From birth we are exposed to judgement of ourselves and others as a standard accompaniment to every aspect of our lives. Judging others has a comfortable, familiar, at-home quality, tempting us to indulge frequently in the pure pleasure of it.

We expend a vast amount of energy in judging ourselves and others, particularly in response to fear-based behaviour. We judge others for their anger, for their self-centredness, their insensitivity, their inconsistency, their greed. All are things for which we judge ourselves.

Closing the heart may also manifest as failing to see the unique beauty of another. When the heart is truly open there is a natural sense of appreciation for others, even while being aware of their imperfections. An early warning sign of the heart's closing is the loss of appreciation. Even though you may not be consciously aware of judging your partner, lack of appreciation dampens the love and the flow of energy between you.

Are we saying judgement is 'bad'? How is one to regard inhumanity, violence? At a more immediate level, how is one to regard the insensitive behaviour of one's partner? Do I need to close my heart when my partner doesn't keep agreements, or isn't tuned into my needs, or gets angry at me unfairly, or treats me insensitively? How is one to respond, in short, when confronted with another's fear?

My own fear presents its case with convincing logic and consummate skill. It asserts that I need judgement to move through the world. If I have a problem with my partner, my discomfort is due to their behaviour. In order to remain safe I must close my heart to them.

My deeper wisdom has a different perspective. If my heart were truly open to my partner at this moment, would there really be a problem? Perhaps, it suggests, the only 'problem' lies in the fact that my heart is closed. To this there is only one solution.

Further, responses arising from a closed heart perpetuate fear, creating more pain and division. The pain in the human consciousness is in urgent need of healing. Judgement does not heal; it perpetuates the very quality that it's judging against. We need to respond to fear-based behaviour without our own fear. Yet it is important to avoid setting up non-judgement as an ideal.

IDEAL AND VISION

Ideals elicit harshness and blame. Whenever I hold an ideal, I will compare my behaviour or another's with my ideal. In most cases I find the behaviour wanting, and berate myself or others for not living up to this ideal. If my ideal is non-judgement, I am going to judge whoever I find being judgemental. Using a harsh means to attain a gentle end, my ego is unaware of its pretence at being spiritual. Fear is once again masquerading as love.

Ego loves to play in spiritual realms, to usurp every important spiritual truth and use it for its own ends. This gives rise to all the forms of spiritual seeking by which we attack others and make them wrong for not following our particular path or living up to our religious ideal.

There is a difference between an ideal and a vision. Holding an ideal so often leads to the closing of the heart in the service of having an open heart – an obvious contradiction. But a vision operates in a different way. When I remember an ideal, I tend to berate myself. When I remember a vision, I have the opportunity to practice it now.

To have a vision of living non-judgementally means that I have seen the beauty of it and deeply wish to live with my heart opened. When I become aware that I have closed my heart, I do not close it further by blaming myself. Rather, I look within to perceive the fear that closed my heart and offer myself the possibility of forgiveness for being afraid.

Ideals place the change in the future. A vision of a changed heart realises it must occur now. Loving means are necessary to a loving end. With an open heart as a vision I practice opening my heart to the best of my ability now, as often as I remember, with no distinction regarding the content.

THE SOURCE OF JUDGEMENT

Why do certain people annoy us, while we overlook others' flaws? The imperfections we react to in others remind us, in however disguised a form, of what we have not forgiven in ourselves. Others become a mirror, showing us an uncomfortable reflection.

If you want to know where your spiritual work lies, consider those people whom you judge the most, who lay beyond the outer limits of your love. They may be individuals or groups: your partner, your parents, former lovers, present and former friends, bosses, teachers; or perhaps certain politicians, sports figures, or authors. Sometimes you judge personality traits such as aggressiveness, passivity, or dishonesty. Sometimes your judgement will extend to whole classes of people: right wing conservatives, 'bleeding heart' liberals, yuppies, men who abuse women, parents who abuse children, hypocrites, victims, hippies, 'the establishment', the military, macho men, wimps, feminists, those who favour the choice of abortion, those opposing abortion, doctors, lawyers, politicians, those in the wrong religion or no religion ... the list is endless. Do you recognise any? We all have our favourite judgements, which we defend with vigour.

We often judge our partner the most. Perhaps our fundamental judgement is that they are not loving us in the way that our ego demands. Ego doubts their love, first because in their humanness they are unable to love us with unconditional, continuous perfection. Second, their love does not always express itself according to our image of what loving behaviour should look like. Of course they judge us similarly for not loving them in the way they want.

Once the original, basic judgement of our partner has occurred we find ourselves looking for and finding a great many little things for which to judge them. Their habits and human imperfections, once easy to overlook, start unaccountably annoying us. Sometimes our partner can scarcely do anything right. Traits which we would forgive in a good friend have become more unforgivable in our partner. The tree of judgement, with its myriad branches, can take up a great deal of space in a relationship, ultimately crowding out the love.

I am in a relationship with a powerful, independent woman who does not always hold my views or want the same thing. In working out her issues, she sometimes displays her human imperfections, which has given me many opportunities to watch my heart close. Sometimes I justify it to myself in the moment; at other times I wish fervently that it were otherwise. My wish for an open heart does not automatically bring it; something more is needed.

THE MOTIVE FOR ELIMINATING JUDGEMENT

The motive for opening the heart has traditionally come from an external authority, such as a religious teacher or teaching. Virtually every religion tells us to love, to be kind, to forgive. If we succeed we are promised future reward in this life or another. If we fail, punishment. But apparently, neither reward, nor punishment, nor commandments seems to have much effect on the deeply rooted habit of judgement. Even strong exhortations to open the heart have little impact. The heart seems to close on its own, without our volition. Heavily rooted conditioning is not going to disappear without some major inner change.

Our heart is more likely to open when our motivation comes from within. Such motivation arises quite naturally when we suspect the immense level of pain that comes, both to us and to those in our lives, from living with a closed heart.

To be in the presence of someone with a closed heart can be painful enough, but to harbour it in oneself is the denial of love, which may be the closest thing we know to hell. I need not believe in the traditional religious concept of hell to experience it in this life. Hell is the world I inhabit when my heart is closed.

In the world of the closed heart I get sidetracked into thinking my happiness comes from having a bank account, a life style, a relationship, good sex, an attractive or healthy body, a fine home, respect from others, and so on. But when I take an honest look at how it has felt after I have achieved whatever I had so ardently coveted, I find the hoped-for state of undisturbed satisfaction always turn rapidly into the usual gnawing discontent.

Nothing in the material world brings any lasting contentment. All the possessions, experiences, pleasures and successes, which I have fervently hoped would bring me relief from my pain, are but ineffective consolation prizes, sooner or later leaving emptiness. All my striving for security, pleasure or power has taken me down a path that leads nowhere. I begin to realise that the largely unconscious value system by which I have led my life is untrue to its core.

To experience the motivation for doing this work requires first that I feel a powerful distaste for the hell of my closed heart, and then that I harness this aversion in the service of my release. The hell is not merely private. The discomfort I feel when my loving relationship turns into hostility or bitterness is related to my feeling when I read about painful and violent conflicts in the troubled areas of the world. It's no different in my relationship from the way it is out in the world. As above so below. The atom has the same basic structure as the solar system; my relational conflict is made of the same stuff as war among nations.

My distaste for all this pain and conflict can lead me to the passionate search for a better way. Earnestness helps, a persistence that won't stop when it meets with obstacles. If I have the intention, I will receive impeccable teachers, teachings, books, experiences, insights – whatever I need.

The return of heaven comes only when the closed heart opens. As I get older it becomes increasingly plain that the only thing I really want, the only thing that will bring me peace, is that I feel love.

Whenever I meet my fear with love, whenever I forgive by releasing my ego, there is a joy that has nothing to do with outer conditions or with the surface fluctuations of my emotional life.

Our hearts have not been very open. Our parents were

211

mostly unable to teach us how. Nor could our religions. Nor the seldom encountered wise elders of our culture. Nor our schools, nor the media. Nor, if we are beyond the early romantic stage, has our intimacy. How, then, can we learn together with our partner to make that elusive transformation from a closed heart to an open one?

OPENING THE CLOSED HEART

The powerful task of opening the heart requires a major inner shift. Simple formulas or mechanical exercises simply don't suffice for this level of transformation. Nevertheless, these guidelines may be of help:

Work On Forgiving Yourself

Your attitude towards your partner is a direct reflection of your attitude towards yourself. You project self-blame outwards as judgement, while forgiveness of yourself softens your response to the other. If you want to love your partner more unconditionally, nothing is more important than working to release your feelings of unworthiness. (*see Chapter 11*)

Accept When Your Heart is Closed

Paradoxically, a major key to opening the heart is accepting when it isn't. When your heart is contracted the temptation is strong to depreciate yourself. But fighting against an undesired trait merely serves to strengthen it. In addition, turning against yourself when your heart has hardened causes you to dislike the people that trigger this feeling. It is easy to get caught up in disliking what triggers your closing down and then blaming yourself for doing that, and so on in an endless pattern of blame.

When your heart is closed to your partner it does not mean that you have stopped loving, although it is true you are not immediately available for certain kinds of interactions. But what a burden to feel obligated to be open to your partner all the time!

You cannot open your heart by an act of will. The heart has its own rhythms of expansion and contraction. When it is expansive it may seem to be fed by a richly flowing river. Other times it feels hard and unmoving. At such times it takes true discipline to stay present and loving to yourself.

Your partner will do a thousand and one things that elicit your judgement, ranging from major offences to the merest hint of a look or a tone of voice. Become familiar with the triggers that close your heart and acknowledge them. The pain of your closed heart is trying to tell you something important which you have not yet learned. And remember the healing will be impeded if you make yourself wrong for judging. By accepting yourself, ego and all, you make it easier to become conscious of your judgements. This is an indispensable step on the way to releasing them. Such acceptance allows you to relax inwardly enough to be able to shift attention from the judgement itself to the mind that is judging. When you explore this mind you will begin to see its own pain, fear and confusion.

Stand Outside Your Judgements

Once your judgements are acknowledged the next step is to put some space around the them, so as not to be totally identified with them. To be identified with a feeling means to be caught up in it. Your feeling or attitude so dominates you that there is no place to stand outside and be aware of it. Listen to people arguing about politics and observe what it is like to be identified with being right. To stop being identified with a feeling means to find an inner place from which to observe it, a place which is itself not part of the feeling. It is important to be aware that you are having feelings while neither justifying nor condemning them.

See Yourself with Honesty

Awareness of oneself has immense power. Because it touches your core, it can transform more deeply than merely trying to live up to ideals. An honest look at yourself, the one who judges, will begin to weaken the belief structure which, through the years, has supported all the judgements.

If at the dinner table you knock over a glass of water, it would be hard to feel righteous towards your partner for their carelessness if they did the same thing a moment later. Most of the things for which we blame our partner are behaviours we do as well, although perhaps in an altered form.

It can be painfully revealing to see that you participate in those very qualities you judge. If you judge my partner for being self-centred, can you honestly say you are not that way? If you judge them for not listening, you need to know if you always listen. If you judge them for being insensitive, you need an honest look at your own sensitivity. If you judge them for being greedy, examine your own level of generosity. Perhaps you judge your partner for not taking your needs more fully into account. Do you always take theirs? If you judge them for all their negative feelings, be honest about whether, in your deepest inner world, you are such a saint. If you judge people for closing their hearts and being unloving, you are probably not aware of the great irony of withholding love because someone has closed their heart. In the act of judging people for being in their ego you are reducing yourself to that same level.

Take a thorough look at yourself when you become aware that you are judging someone. Pay attention to your heart, to whether or not if feels genuinely good to be judging. Pay attention to the hidden assumptions of moral superiority which underlie the judgement. Observe how you are feeling about yourself. Perhaps you will become aware of the feeling of inadequacy lying underneath the judgement. Instead of trying to change the content of your judgemental thoughts, shift your attention to your painful feeling of unworthiness. Now you are addressing the root cause of the judging.

As you observe yourself in this fashion over time, it becomes increasingly hard to support your judgements with your intellect. Before self-examination you had not only passed judgement, you justified it as well. But now there is a useful dichotomy between your emotions and your intellect. When you cease believing in the righteousness of your judgements, an inner circuit is broken. You are in the peculiar position of harbouring feelings in whose foundation you now have grave doubt. A process of erosion is taking place. The voice of fear, challenged to its very core, is no longer the only force operating within the mind. Through persistence in the process you may find the habit of judgement begins to lose the power of its hold.

SEE DIFFICULT BEHAVIOUR AS A CALL FOR HELP

Think for a moment about your partner when they are behaving in a way that you find distasteful. See if it is possible to perceive their behaviour as an expression of fear and pain. Out of that fear they are being aggressive, or they are withdrawing, or they are being dishonest, or self-centred, or sexually inappropriate, or they are not listening, or however else their fear is manifesting. Consider that they were simply a hurt, scared child, in need at that moment of nothing other than compassion. Of course, your compassion allows for making firm boundaries when needed.

Take it a step further. Imagine your partner were an ally in a scenario you were creating together, bringing you both the very teaching required to release a particular obstacle to the expression of your love. Every time your partner acts unlovingly, if you are able to see it as a call for help rather than as a threat, and respond accordingly, you have been graced with additional love into your life. In addition, through your more loving response, something in both of you is healed.

A temptation exists to hold in your mind an image of your partner in their fearful aspect, to believe that their ego is who they are. But the basic feeling you hold towards your partner tends to bring out that very quality in them. Whenever you

215

think about your partner, try to look beyond the surface manifestations of fear and penetrate right through to the core of who they really are. See them as a being of divine origin, who may be momentarily caught up in confusion and fear, and who therefore deserves compassion.

It does not really matter if you have forgotten about this perspective for a few minutes or hours or months or years or decades. At this moment you have an opportunity to release the past.

It's been just as tough for your partner as it has for you. They have gone through just as much pain and fear as you have. Like you, they are doing the best they can. Each moment of pain is an opportunity to find compassion for both of you for all the suffering inherent in this whole process.

The fearful mind continually suggests that it is not safe to love and there is good cause to close the heart. But for Martha and I, in our moments of clarity, one truth stands out above all else: we are not in danger from our partner's ego. The only thing that feels danger is our own ego. There is never any justification for closing our heart to our partner.

One of the great challenges of my life and of my relationship with Martha is taking this idea and actually putting it into practice. If Martha snaps at me, my main interest is to avoid the temptation to withdraw or attack, and instead see that she is in pain, afraid, and that the only appropriate response is compassion.

If you have tried, you know that this is a most difficult challenge. Learning to open my heart when it wants to close has been the most arduous lesson of my life. Although these ideas and practices have been helpful in softening the rough edges, there have been times when things between Martha and I became so filled with hostility that we hadn't the personal resources to cope. When it becomes this murky and confusing none of our usual tools and techniques seems sufficient.

ASK FOR HELP

At such times there is a resource available that operates at a totally different level from the limited ego mind. This resource is accessible at any time for the asking. Native Americans call it Great Spirit; the Christian tradition calls it the Holy Spirit. This deeper wisdom lives within each being, knowing the truth of every situation, and can only be appreciated through direct experience.

At the physical level the deeper wisdom functions quite efficiently underneath conscious awareness, providing with inspiring precision the trillions of biochemical responses necessary to digest our food, nourish our cells, move our muscles, and heal our wounds. At the mental level this same wisdom is available to guide, comfort and inspire, and to help us move towards harmony and peace.

When a couple is at an impasse or in a serious argument, resolution may seem impossibly difficult. Each person is locked fiercely into their own position of being right and neither wants to let go, despite the obvious pain involved. Whenever Martha and I are enmired in such a place it feels beyond our ability to escape.

These are the moments for us to make use of this deeper wisdom and ask for help. And we find that whenever we do ask, help invariably arrives.

The only difficulty lies in getting to that point where we are willing to ask. The magnitude of this challenge should not be underestimated. When I am so completely enmeshed with Martha in an angry, blaming state, my ego has absolutely no interest in love, peace, or resolution. Ego most decidedly prefers to be right, even at the cost of remaining miserable. Asking for help is the last thing in the world it wants.

If my entire being were imprisoned in this view there would indeed be no hope. But buried deep within lies a place untouched by ego, remaining with enough clarity to suspect the ego's view of the situation is untrue. A small fragment of my awareness is willing to be released from the ego's stranglehold, is willing to step outside the painful prison of attack and defence. Somewhere within lurks a little bit of willingness to see by a different light.

When I am holding on tightly to the source of my pain, the most difficult task is locating that one per cent which is willing to let go. It sometimes takes a supreme effort of stretching to find that willingness. The other ninety-nine per cent is loud, insistent, overwhelming and is convinced there is nothing else. However, this is not a struggle between the two. Nothing is ever accomplished by fighting against the ego. The only worthwhile struggle lies in locating the willingness to abandon the battlefield. The inner act by which you find this little willingness cannot really be described in words, but it is worth learning how, for in this lies release from relational suffering.

If one of you has been able to locate the little willingness not to be in the ego, they can request that their partner join in asking for help. Pause for a moment to get in touch with the part of you that is willing to receive help. Whoever first suggested it might ask the greater wisdom, in whatever vocabulary is suitable, to help the two of you release your limited perspective and see the situation through different eyes.

Sit together for a while in silence. Let go for an instant of your entire history, whether it be a minute ago or twenty years. Experience together a moment where thought and conflict have ceased, where the mind is empty and receptive to what lies beyond its chattering. It is as if this timeless moment were the only instant that ever existed. It does not matter if the cave had been dark for 10,000 years; if you light a match the cave is now light and the duration of its previous darkness is irrelevant.

This silent asking can bring a miraculous shift. In one second the endlessly complex tangle of despair and blame can be transformed, the ancient darkness wiped away and a blessing take its place. No matter how much pain and confusion you have created together, it can all evaporate in a single instant of love.

There is great beauty every time you perform this fundamental spiritual gesture. Through it you keep learning anew that all healing takes place now, with an ease totally independent of the pain's seeming strength.

I once heard a person being interviewed who had been very heavily addicted to heroin and had successfuly freed himself from the habit. The interviewer was impressed: 'It must have taken some heroic effort to overcome such a powerful addiction. Tell me, how long did it take you to kick the habit?' The former addict instantly replied, 'Oh, about one second.'

On many an occasion Martha and I have invited the deeper wisdom when it seemed beyond our capacity to free ourselves from the toxicity we had created. Healing has always graced us, no matter how seemingly hopeless the situation. The very intention to receive help aligns us with something greater than our limited minds and creates an environment where it can enter into our awareness. Healing may arrive in various forms. After asking for help, Martha and I look up and often find the other smiling. The clouds have simply parted and it's over. Sometimes one or both will receive a revelation which allows us to see the situation in a fresh light. Often it comes wordlessly. Although the truth may arrive in different fashions, it always comes.

SUMMARISING

To open the closed heart you first focus on yourself: releasing feelings of unworthiness, accepting when your heart is closed, putting space around the judgements and seeing yourself more clearly and honestly. The next step focuses the same clear light on the one who is eliciting the judgement, in an attempt to see them with more compassion. The final step turns attention to an energy beyond the limited confines of the mind, inviting it in to perform its healing. This is not a linear progression. The work is done in all areas simultaneously.

It is not that this process will immediately bring an end to all judgement. The mind's habit of closing the heart is tenacious, and the ego will persist in its ancient ways. You will doubtless fall down many times. Nevertheless, a change eventually begins, perhaps at first scarcely noticeable. Something has altered. A new vigilance persists under the surface, one that quickly spots the old inner habits as they arise and in whose light they quietly dissolve. Primitive patterns of attack and defence do not have a chance to take hold the way they once did. The slightest tightening in the body, negative thought, or closing of the heart sets off a warning light, an immediate invitation to investigate the attitude behind the contraction.

A miracle takes place when two people sanctify their relationship to the lofty task of opening the closed heart. An extraordinary process is begun that goes far beyond what is possible with just one person. Once you set foot on this path the universe will grace you with creative ways to see things differently, to release weary habits, to reinterpret in a new light what happens between you. It will send you tests, difficulties, obstacles of the highest order. But you will also receive many encouraging and satisfying reminders that you are on a path in harmony with the highest good for all.